TEX SMITH'S HOW TO BUILD
CUSTOM CARS
MOST EVERYTHING ABOUT CUSTOMS!

by LeRoi Tex Smith

Motorbooks International
Publishers & Wholesalers
®

First published in 1989 by Motorbooks International Publishers and Wholesalers, PO Box 2, 729 Prospect Avenue, Osceola, WI 54020, USA.

Motorbooks International books are also available at discounts in bulk quantity for industrial or sales-promotional use. For details, write to Special Sales Manager at the Publisher's address.

Library of Congress Cataloging-in-Publication Data
ISBN 0-87938-397-6

Printed and bound in the United States of America.

CONTENTS

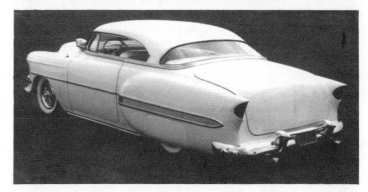

FOREWORD

P lease, indulge me. Make allowance for my old-timey ways. Having greying hair and becoming long of tooth, I still spell Custom Car with a C. I know that lots of people think it should be with a K, as in Kustoms by Barris, but for me any time I see the K, I immediately associate the car with George or Sam. So much for age and wisdom and all that rot.

This is a book about custom cars. It is a book about Kustom Kars. It is not a book about lowriders. A custom/kustom might be a lowrider, but a lowrider is not necessarily a custom/kustom.

A custom car is a vehicle (truck/passenger car/whatever) that has been changed/personalized to meet the desires of the owner. A very simple definition, yet one that can become hazy almost immediately.

Is a personalized 1934 Ford a custom? Is a wildy modified 1983 coupe a custom? The answer can be yes or no. It all depends. Must a custom have skirts? A chopped top? All trim removed? It all depends.

And this is what makes the custom so absolutely unique. So neat. So bitchin'. So.....well, personal.

A custom is whatever the owner wants it to be. It doesn't have to meet some rigid standard as set by someone else. It doesn't have to be a chopped 1950 Mercury convertible. It doesn't have to cost ten zillion dollars. It doesn't have to appeal to everyone. It does have to make the owner happy. That's all. Yes, a lowrider does all these things, but there really is a difference.

To paraphrase a term used in street rodding, Customs aren't about winning for losing...they are about fun! If you're only into customs as a way to furnish the trophy room, you are probably going to be disappointed. Not about the trophies, but about missing out on the great joy of just cruising in a special vehicle.

Customs are, after all, for driving. For cruising. For having a cool time. Hot rods are for making Banzai runs down the salt flats or the drag strip, or for putting the gee-whiz on the gas station crowd. Customs are for cruising main street, for making a low and slow pass on the drive-in, for proving beyond any doubt that art as sculpture can absolutely be accomplished with rubber and plastic and metal. To own a custom, to drive a custom is to be a winner. Period. A custom does not need to be entirely handbuilt by the owner to still be a personal statement. If you're talented enough to do your own work, that's wonderful. A custom project is an excellent place to learn about metal and upholstery and engines.

A custom does not need to be radically different. It can be very mild, and still be totally effective. It does not need to be completely finished (if any custom or hot rod ever is really finished), it can have primer spots, or areas of work, and still be a custom. It can be a daily driver, or tucked away and used on rare occasion. Because a custom is whatever the owner wants it to be.

Lots of customs are superior examples of art, others have glaring fzg process. I know of no professional customizer who isn't a bit dissatisfied with a vehicle. An improvement could be made here, a change there would help a line flow more smoothly, the color could be more subtle. A custom is never finished, therefore it is a learning process. For the pro as well as the novice.

Currently there are over 5000 members of the Kustom Kemps of America. Compare this to over 40,000 members of the National Street Rod Association. Yet, not so many years ago, there were ten custom cars to every hot rod on the street. That ratio can, and will, return. How fast will be the ressurection is mostly a matter of awzareness. If the hobby gets the national magazine attention it deserves, the resurgence of the custom will be very rapid. The

July 1989 Hot Rod Magazine has excellent coverage of the Billy Gibbons Cadillac. A radical machine, this car will probably grace the cover of a ZZ Top record album, and it will do wonders to get younger people interested in custom cars. They may not flock to the more traditional styles of shoebox Fords and Mercs, but they will come to understand that a personal statement can only be made with something personal. Not a factory BMW or Camaro. Nothing personal there. Not a pro-fat street machine just like 12 others in town. Nothing personal there.

Custom cars are beginning to show in international advertising, just as street rods did about 15 years ago, and this will most assuredly focus more attention on the hobby. But, and this is very important, anyone can spot a hot rod. Very few people are knowledgeable enough about cars to know that a custom is not just some kind of zooty old car. This means that the more customs get on the street, the more the average person will come to recognize a custom from just an unremembered car that somehow seems to look better today.

Perhaps the neatest thing about owning a custom is being able to enjoy it day in-day out, every day of the year. Not so possible with a hot rod. This single fact of use may be why we all loved customs so much in the late 40s and early 50s. Back then, an A-V8 Ford was just a used car. It usually cost about $15 for a Model A Ford (still in great condition), and another $50 or so to install a flathead V8 engine. But the custom guys were on the streets with new cars. Cars that were comfortable, cars that were reliable, cars that got all the girl attention! If it was a question of cruising Main in an open roadster or a nice warm Merc, you just know who got the girl.

So every car nut wanted a hot rod for boiling the blood, and a custom (also for boiling the blood). It was never a question of having a hot rod and a new car. New cars were for nerds, the dorks who drove their dad's lime green four door Flush-O-Matic. Customs might be new cars, but new cars were never customs. Get the drift? Well, you hadda be there to understand, maybe.

Another neat thing about a custom is that it isn't expected to be a maxi-performance automobile. Nope, that is for the hot rods. Customs are for cruising, man. Cool, slow, sleek, snakey. But

they gotta look just right, and they gotta sound just right.. The wrong exhaust note and a drooler is a dud.

Of course, once in awhile there come along the custom that can put most any fast car on the trailer. These are the really far out wheels, because they are kind of the ultimate sleepers. You know, a new car can be all hopped up secretly and do a number on the road, and be a sleeper. But a sled? A sled that can run hard is really a top dog.

I saw my first custom cars before WW II, in California. Before that, in Oklahoma and Texas I had seen strip-downs, but never a custom. By the end of War Two, my dad's body shop was getting a smattering of customs. So were lots of other shops, but most bodymen didn't want to do specialized work. Work that ranged all the way from radical top chops to not-so-simple hood shaving to really simple lowering. For one buck a side, we would light up the gas torch and heat the rear springs to whatever taildragging height you desired! Instant cool, instant cruiser. True, a neck snapper, but who cared? Long shackles cost a bit more.

It was during those special years in Northern California that I learned of guys like Gil Ayala and the Barris boys and Bailon and Summers and...gee, the list just seems endless. Some of them are still around, most are still very much interested in customs. Lots of these early builders went on to create Hollywood movie and TV stuff, others drifted over into hot rods, but just about everyone still has a fond place for the customs. They were, and are, superb ways to make a personal statement.

This book is more about the body and the paint and all the stuff that readily identifies a custom car, than it is about the engine. In fact, we just touch on engines and transmissions and rearends. Because what you do with these particular elements is so very well covered in other books and magazines. Here, we're trying to concentrate on the unique part of a custom.

But the bottom line to all of this is still the simple truth: A custom is whatever the owner wants. It can kinda be a lowrider, and it can kinda be a hot rod,, and it can kinda be a pro-streeter. But above all, it has to look just right. It has to sound just right. It has to move just right. These are all intangibles, to be sure, but they are part and parcel of every real custom car ever built. Since the first wagon body was bolted to a self-propelled chassis.

Finally, be advised that there is no way possible for us to jam everything about building a custom into one book of just over 200 pages. When we got out the pencil to do our preliminary planning, we found very quickly that such an all-encompassing book would take well over 1000 pages. That's one-thousand, folks! So, rather than do the impossible, we elected to make this a series. What you hold in your hands is Volume 1. There will be Volumes 2, and 3, and more. By the time we're through a half-dozen, we should have covered the subject. And, we want to call your attention to our companion, CUSTOM CAR MAGAZINE. This is a bi-monthly that is about customs only, nothing but customs. No rods, no race cars, nothing but customs. We can't cover every aspect of building a custom car in CCM, either. But we can, and do, get the reader up to speed on what is happening in the hobby/sport.

See you on the streets!

LeRoi Tex Smith

The mists of time have veiled the answer, but there aren't many people asking the question anyway: When was the first custom car created. If the first hot rod happened when someone decided to removed the fenders and windshield from an old flivver, then surely the very first custom was when someone decided to change the body style (however slightly). In a way, the words (and meanings) custom and hot rod are very much intertwined with history and the automobile.

Let's assume that the coachbuilders were really the first people to do custom work. These were the companies set up to do specialty bodies on factory chassis, and they began to appear at the same time cars appeared. In fact, most of these companies were building special bodies for horse-drawn vehicles before cars came along, the reason for the term coachbuilder.

The coachbuilder worked almost exactly like the modern customizer. The customer would wander into the offices with a few ideas on what was wanted, but very little idea how the body could be built. From these "one-off's", the coachbuilder could increase volume and become a specialty body supplier to the factory. Today, 1most customizers build one car at a time, but sometimes there is an order for several cars, perhaps even hundreds. So, the distance between a famous coachbuilder of the 1920s and a famous (or not so famous customizer of the 1990s may be only a matter of years, not of product.

This hasn't always been the case, however. Early on, the customizer tended to be an individual with a talent to work sheetmetal. Only the barest necessities were available in the line of tools and materials, and the end products were usually minimal changes to Bodystyle. A bodyman working in a small garage in East Overshoe simply did not have the wealth of experience, equipment, training, and materials available to the modern metalsmith. Therefore, the results were usually quite modest. Fender skirts, grille covers, solid hood panels .seldom did these people try top chops or sections or grille changes.

Today, even the most amateur customizer can tackle a major body change with a reasonable expectation of getting good results. The "cold" welders have helped immensely, as have the improved plastic fillers and the special two-part paints. But mostly, today there is an abundance of information on how to do different custom techniques.

Lots of information, but it hasn't been readily available unless the builder was in contact with other builders, such as at the custom runs and shows. Because published information all but disappeared about 1965, when the modern custom era went into hiding. Between 1950 and 1965, there were a number of monthly and annual magazines/books that featured custom car material. All of this began to disappear as the Detroit factory hot rod began to hit the streets. Traditional hot rods were rapidly displaced by the hot factory cars in the early Sixties. The customs followed, but at a slower pace, so that by the end of the 1960s about the only place to see a custom was in a show. Not because rods and customs were any the less highly desirable as individual statements. The reason they were supplanted by factory machinery was simple economics. For only a few dollars down, the hot rodder could buy a new car with far more performance and comfort than the traditional hot rod. At the same time, the new cars were beginning to come with all the styling tricks of the traditional custom...lower tops, thinner body lines, trick grilles, wild interiors, etc, etc, etc. In short, the car enthusiast could have a car that was both rod and custom, and it was new!

The current ressuregence of interest in custom cars has served to unveil an interesting fact...there are literally thousands of custom car enthusiasts "out there" who never really disappeared. They just became invisible. Where a community at one time might have had hundreds of customs, that number had dwindled to only a handful by the early 1980s. And the "names" of customizing were unknown to the new generations of car nuts. Names like Harry Westergaard, Jimmy Summers, Gil Ayala, Link Paola, Joe Bailon, Cushenberry, Winfield, Barris, Wilhelm, Farhner, Starbird, Jeffries, Puhl, the Alexander Brothers, Valley Custom.......history. Ancient history. There were dozens more around the country, outstanding custom builders who never got the noteriety of these people. Some of them have survived, to greet the new wave of enthusiasm.

Individual customizers tended to spring up in the shadow of the more established coachbuilding firms, at least before World War II. Because southern California was a literally hot bed of specialty car interest, when firms such as Bowman & Schwartz would do a really outstanding car for a movie idol# it was not unreasonable to think that a "lesser" individual might get a knowledgeable bodyman to create something a bit less extravagant. Thus it was inevitible that southern California would spawn hundreds of customs cars before WW II, and thousands afterward.

As hot rodding began to spread across the nation, thanks in large part to new magazines like HOT ROD, customs went along for the ride. Almost overnight, customs were to be seen everywhere, so that by the mid-1950s it wasn't uncommon to find quality custom cars everywhere in the U.S. and Canada. Of course, many of them were bought from the west coast, but local customizers were flexing their creative muscles as well. Custom car shows were proliferating by the early 1960s, and if there were a Golden Age of customizing it would have been the period 1961-1963. This was when some truly outstanding designs were being created. In southern California, in Detroit, in Chicago, on the east coast. Yes, there were some awesome vehicles built before that time, but never so many in such a short period of time. A large number of these cars were created just for the car show circuit, or for specialty use in movies/tv. Some were built just as promotional tools for plastic model kit companies. And some were just the results of a very fertile imagination, such as the many vehicles out of the shop of Ed Roth.

Almost as quickly as this dynamic period was born, it was gone. As mentioned, done in by Detroit.

But everything that happens generates a history, and customizing is no exception. Today, there is a huge groundswell of nostalgic interest in customs, and to be expected much of this interest is from people who were teen agers in the 50s and 60s. Old customs are being found and ressurected, customizers from that period are trying to find some of their old projects to rebuild, new customs are being built as clones of original designs. But, more importantly, a solid wave of new customs are being built. Some are in the traditional vein, while some, such as ZZ Top's Billy Gibbons' Cadillac, is spawning creativity heretofor unseen. Customs have a history, all right, and it is now!!!

The history of customizing is graphically illustrated here, with examples from Winfield in the '50s/'60s, and the '40 Ford by Harry Westergaard in the late '40s, early '50s. Than, as now, the custom was expression of personal taste in automotive design.

Only the Mercury two door at the bottom is a reflection of the older custom, note the smoothie caps, wide whites, and absence of running boards. Dean Bachelor went on from this car to edit Road & Track magazine for many years, Winfield built the Merc at left and is still building outstanding specialty cars. The pickup is from the '70s, the two cars at top are as modern as any custom can be.

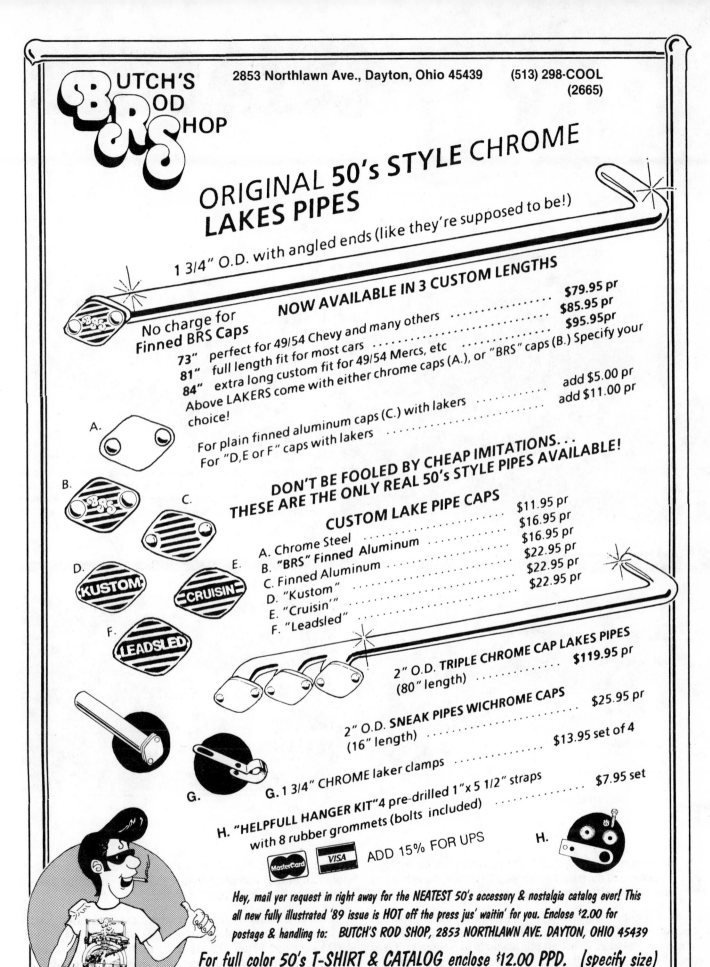

CHASSIS

Here's a chassis swap for a Mercury, using a late model GM product. The entire GM floorpan and lower area of the firewall is used. This can be done by an amateur with most basic of tools, lots of patience.

Chassis

T he custom cars being built today are better, on the average, than those of the past. The bodywork is better, the upholstery and paint are better, and for certain, the chassis is better.

Much of this improvement has to do with better suspension and brakes, and a lot of it is due to superior engineering in small areas such as noise isolation. What all this amounts to is simple: If you want to have a ride with all the charm of yesterday mixed with the engineering of today, you can. But it is work, and it does require

some planning. Fortunately, there has been a tremendous amount of experimenting during the last 5 years, and today's custom builder can capitalize on this.

There is a rather vague point where the "modern" chassis took over from the "old" chassis. This was about 1949. Some GM cars had better chassis prior to this, some cars didn't really get updated until later. For the most part, this was when the independent front suspension came to all American cars, and it made a significant difference in how the cars rode. The wheelbases had been gradually increasing since the late 1930s, and rear springs were getting longer and "softer". Tube shock absorbers completed the improvements. Interestingly, it wasn't until the radial that tires made great changes in vehicle handling and ride. Unfortunately, the brakes did not improve as rapidly as other parts of the suspension, and it was not until the late 1960s that disc brakes put the finishing touches on the American car chassis. Without a really serious threat from imported cars, the American builders delayed improvements as long as possible. The pre-1949 Ford custom will have a good frame, but a really antique suspension system and brakes that are poor at best. The pre-1949 GM vehicles used an improved independent front suspension and semi-elleptic rear springs that had been steadily advancing since the late 1930s. Even though these systems are useable, they do not begin to compare to late model suspensions.

For the pre-49 Ford products, it is possible to use Chrysler type torsion bar suspensions from the mid-size MoPars of the late 60s and early 70s. There is a kit available from Gibbon Mfg to make these units a bolt-in. It is also possible to use the popular Pinto/Mustang front end in these cars. At the rear, semi-elleptic spring kits allow the use of a variety of open driveline rearends. All of these items are available through many different street rod sources (check out our Hot Rod Mechanix magazine).

Things are not so good for the pre-1949 GM products, or early MoPar products. Since these vehicles already have IFS, most

builders confine their changes to disc brakes. Kits for these swaps are scarce (or non-existent), so some suppliers are beginning to offer the Pinto/Mustang front end conversion. As of this writing, we know of no dropped spindles for these early GM or MoPar products.

Things are not a great deal better for vehicles produced from 1949 to about 1955, as far as dropped front spindles or disc brake kits are concerned. After 1955, product availability improves markedly, and as a general rule there is little or no need to do major frame/suspension changes to a post-1955 car. Other than adding disc brakes up front.

It is in the 1949-55 area where some really exciting frame and suspension work has been going on. In this section, we include a great article on modifying the Chevelle frame to fit under 1948 and earlier Ford products. This same procedure can be used for practically any pre-49 vehicle. We also include a piece on using the cross-chassis torsion bar Volare front end. While we show it going under a pickup, it works as well under any vehicle. The only problem will be front tire track width, and if a person really wanted to do some work in narrowing the unit, it would be a dynamite addition to any early custom...because the torsion bars are adjustable and the front could be raised or lowered at will. Incidentally, this Volare front end is being widely used by owners of custom pickups of the 1950s and 1960s. And, we include information about putting the late model GM chassis under cars such as the '49-'54 Merc.

There seems to be no end to great possibilities in improving the chassis for traditional customs.

The chassis/flooring swap is very good on body that has rusted original floor The body can be channeled at this time, the Merc shown is dropped about 4 inches over the frame/flooring and new sections of sheet metal added between old body/late frame. Entire area around perimeter of the body/floor must be welded solid.

Frame Clips

A number of years ago, an enterprising customizer in southern California figured out how to mate a late model GM front frame section to the Ford F-oo frame. Instant independent suspension with disc brakes, and the truck could be lowered at the same time. Overnight the change was a sensation, and that particular shop was doing as many as 5 frame clips a day. Not long afterward, the same shop added the late frame clip to an early Chevy, the swap was covered in a magazine, and the rest is history.

It is not a difficult job to mate a Chevelle front frame clip to something like a 1949-later Ford product, or a similar GM product. The late model clip is cut right at the firewall, where the frame rails straighten out toward the rear. Measure the centerline of this suspension between wheels and where the frame is severed. Duplicate this measurement to the original chassis being worked on, and cut that frame. Slide the new frame into place. Of course, the car frame needs to be level, and supported just back of where the frame is cut off. The new frame is leveled from side to side and fore/aft and set in place. In most cases, the Chevelle clip aligns very closely with the older car frame, so that only pieces of heavy plate stock are needed to put everything together. The idea is to never skimp here...make this junction strong and with plenty of gusset.

At this time, the front of the car can be made lower simply by welding the frame clip higher on the original frame. Do some careful measuring of the original car height and the Chevelle height to determine where the new clip will be welded in place. It is essential to make this welded junction super strong, and it is necessary to do some diagonal measurements during construction to make sure the chassis is square. When a late frame clip is added, new frame horns must be built, along with new radiator core mounting points. The fender splash aprons must be trimmed to fit, or new aprons fabricated. Check the article on the Buick (under Examples) to see how such a graft takes place. When a frame clip is used, motor mounts are already in place for a Chevy and the steering gearbox is in place. Use a clip with disc brakes, and even that area of original car weakness is eliminated.

Frame Swaps

The really terrific frame/suspension update is possible when a complete late model chassis is used. This got started a number of years ago when Dick Dean started making the full swaps in his southern California shop.

Dean prefers to use the mid-size Olds chassis of the late 1960s/early 1970s. These chassis have a 118-inch wheelbase (as do the 1969-73 Pontiac Grand Prix), which is exactly what the

1949-later Mercury has. But Dean goes everyone a step better. While it is possible to just drop the Mercury body onto the bare GM chassis, Dean cuts out the original Mercury flooring and much of the Mercury firewall. The GM floor is cut from the donor body and the GM firewall is trimmed around the perimeter, leaving the steering and brake pedal assembly in place. In essence, only the wiring that is fastened to the GM fender splash apron is removed and laid over on the GM engine. Even the seats and gas tank of the GM unit are left in place.

The bottomless Mercury body is lowered in place and the Merc rear fenders aligned with the GM wheels. This places the firewall in almost exact original Mercury position, so the firewall is trimmed to allow the body to set down on the GM flooring. When everything is aligned, the Mercury body is welded to the GM floor, and the trimmed GM firewall is welded to the Mercury body. Instant swap. The frame horns must be modified to accept the Mercury bumper (or whatever bumper is to be used), and the radiator core support is welded to the crossmember. Mercury splash panels are trimmed to clear the GM suspension.

This frame swap can be accomplished very rapidly, and the results are very gratifying, especially since the late GM seats can be used, as well as the entire steering assembly and brake assembly. Even the full wiring harness all the firewall can be modified to fit the early dash. With some careful trimming and fitting, the late GM heater/air conditioner will fit under the dash.

Obviously, the same kind of frame/flooring swap can be done on other cars, the key is to match wheelbases. This swap is especially appealing to someone with an early body that has the flooring rusted badly. Such was Paul Beckstrand of Wildwood, N.J. Paul had a 1950 Mercury with a very rough body in the flooring area. Badly rusted, it was a perfect candidate for a frame/floor swap.

The wheelbase on the Mercury is 118-inches, which is the same as an Oldsmobile 98 Regency (1977 model) four door and a Buick Park Avenue. Paul hung the body in the air with a couple of Come-A-Longs, suspended over the Old chassis and floor pan. Working from the rear wheel location, he trimmed the Olds floor and Mercury floor sheet metal a bit at a time, trying the fit, until he had the body channeled 4 inches below the Olds flooring. Paul did all the work alone, and reports it wasn't difficult. Only required a lot of patience. He does report that since the Olds tread width is slightly greater than the Mercury, the channel may cause slight wheel/tire interference. Solution to this will be a positive offset wheel.

Here the quarter panel of a badly rusted Merc body has been cut away for later replacement, this exposes area of body inner structure that can be beefed up and welded to the G flooring. The idea is to make things stronger than necessary (seemingly), and they will turn out just about right. After all welding is done, it is a good idea to fill all the seams/cracks with body caulk.

The body is suspended over the late GM chassis, rear wheel opening is aligned with rear wheels. The chassis/floor in this case is an Oldsmobile. The Olds firewall is trimmed just above the frame (arrow) and the Mercury firewall is trimmed to match, then everything is welded together. In some cases, the entire GM firewall is retained.

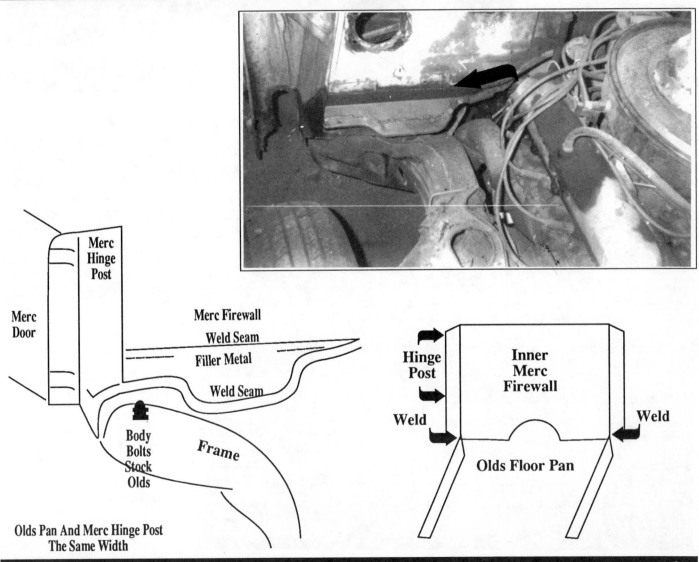

Merc Hinge Post

Merc Door

Merc Firewall

Weld Seam

Filler Metal

Weld Seam

Body Bolts Stock Olds

Frame

Olds Pan And Merc Hinge Post The Same Width

Hinge Post

Weld

Inner Merc Firewall

Weld

Olds Floor Pan

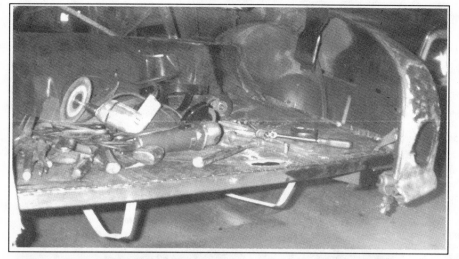

Note how the Mercury body rear lip is now well below the floor level, a product of the channel. Sections of sheetmetal must be cut and fit between the Mercury body and GM flooring, again it is vital that there be no gaps anywhere.

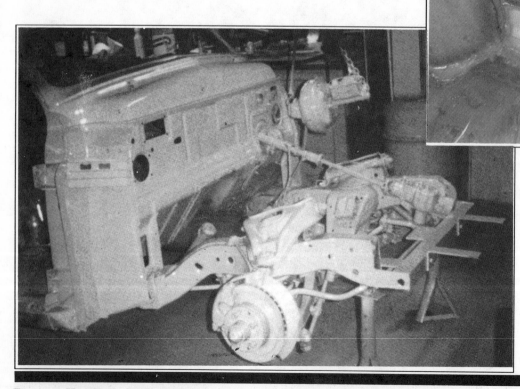

The frame horns must be reshaped to accept the radiator core support, new bracket must be made for the front bumper. Note how nicely the late GM steering column enters the fire-wall. This same frame swap is possible with most older cars, no matter what make/model. The key is matching the wheelbase.

'49 to '51 Mercury Chassis Swap Using 66-68 Mid GM or 69-72 GM

By Gerry Charvat

This can be accomplished by doing the same steps as 41-48 Ford except extending wheelbase to 118". The 4 door 115" chassis is best to use, also 65-67 with straight frame 5 horn are the best to modify.

At the rear graft the old Merc rear section to the G.M. frame this allows use of Merc gas tank in stock location, also spare tire well remains stock. The rear bumper bolts on as original.

The mid G.M. side rails can be left intact by triming a small body section at fire wall mounting area. Or you can trim the frame corners and add an angle mount, thus eliminating all side rail modifications, except stretching 3"

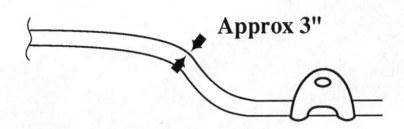

Approx 3"

At the front frame horns a bracket is added to mount the front bumper.

Front

A cross bar using 2 x 2 x 1/4 angle to mount Merc radiator horseshoe, giving dog house alignment as original Merc.

Using this method the inner fender panel may be trimed and still leave freash air tubes in place, allowing use of stock heater/defroster system

All other systems, power brakes tilt column, and pedals fit nicely as they were to be.

NOTES: I use early 80 full size G.M. pedals and 9" power brake units. Also use colums with shaft to steering box (check spline size, some differ in diameter).

Buick and Pontiac chassis set lower than Chevy & Olds.

Late Chassis For Early Bodies —

We're talking super zoomie and double-throw-down trick here, folks, this is the GM 4-door mid-size 115-inch wheelbase frame(late 60's, early 70's), with side rails modified for the Fat Ford crowd. Stock Chevelle exhaust system bolts in, front frame horns must be modified for chosen radiator support.

by Gerry Charvat

I made an innocent mistake. I sent along a few photos of my Ford convertible to Tex Smith. I mean, the blue car with the modified Chevelle chassis. From there, it all went into some other dimension. The questions were like: "Got any photos?", or "Do you have the measurements?", and "Can you send that stuff along, with some technical information, so we can share it in this volume?" (I shudda stood in my shop and not answered the phone.)

The really neat thing about this swap is that anyone with welding ability can do it, and end up with a very inexpensive modern chassis. Very safe, with super handling,

and you have the neat options of GM power steering, great brakes, modern electrical system, etc. I have a rod/custom building shop, and one customer said, "This car is going together so fast it is spooky!" Whatever, if you want a set of drawings and instructions, with a materials list, I sell that for $50 ('41-'48 Ford only). Of course, if I get enough interest, I'll even make up material kits. If I do a chassis in my shop, the price breakdown is like this: Completely rebuilt, ready for body, all new component innards...$3295; Modified chassis only, no component rebuild... $1595; Modify customer chassis, no component rebuild...$1195, etc. Give me a call at (219)482-7473. But back to Tex's needs.

I scrounged all over the place for photographs, never having intended to do a professional photo layout, and I include them here, along with a sketch of the modified frame. This is different from the type of frame/chassis swap Dick Dean does on the west coast for 1949 and later Mercs, in that he has to make practically no frame modifications. Here, we have to work up a new central frame section. But, it isn't very difficult. All you need remember is to make all of the welds very good, and use strong gussets. Measure and re-measure as you proceed, and you won't get into trouble. Good luck!

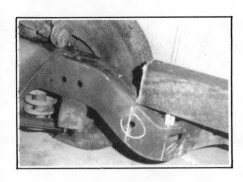

Left - Once GM chassis is stripped, locate two pieces of 3x4-inch, 1/8-inch tubing that is 6 foot 2 inches to "straighten" perimeter frame.

Center - This hole is 11 1/2 inches behind front crossmember and is measuring starting point. Actual cut will be 5-6 inches behind this, giving an overlapping flap.

Right - New frame insert is laid on top stock frame and lines drawn for cutting guide.

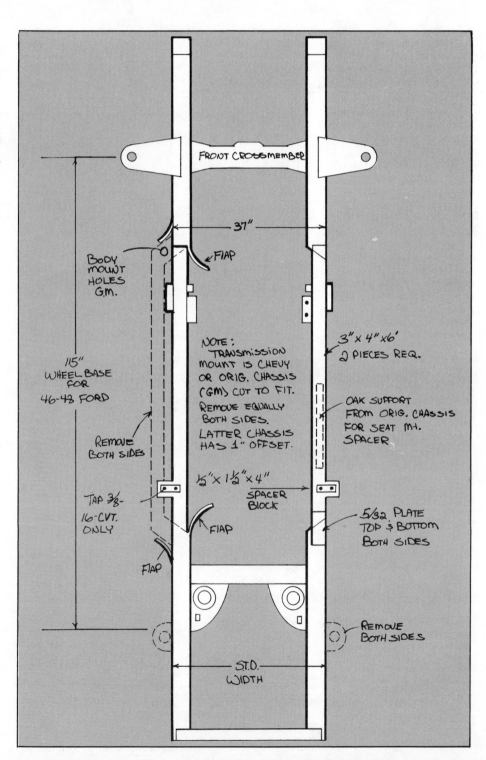

FRONT CROSSMEMBER

37"

FLAP

BODY MOUNT HOLES G.M.

NOTE:
TRANSMISSION MOUNT IS CHEVY OR ORIG. CHASSIS (GM) CUT TO FIT. REMOVE EQUALLY BOTH SIDES. LATTER CHASSIS HAS 1" OFFSET.

3" x 4" x 6' 2 PIECES REQ.

OAK SUPPORT FROM ORIG. CHASSIS FOR SEAT MT. SPACER

115" WHEEL BASE FOR 46-48 FORD

REMOVE BOTH SIDES

½" x 1½" x 4" SPACER BLOCK

TAP ⅜-16-CVT. ONLY

5/32 PLATE TOP & BOTTOM BOTH SIDES

FLAP

FLAP

REMOVE BOTH SIDES

ST.D. WIDTH

Above - Rear frame extensions must be shortened, for the 1941-48 Fords this final distance will be 32 1/2 inches from centerline of rear axle to rear of the frame extension. On some chassis, there will be a 3-inch upward curve at the rear of this extension. More on this later.

Above - Overlap flaps on inside and outside of the rail insert piece insure maximum strength for the area. Additional plate can be made for the top of the rail junctures front and back, if desired. Such plates are definitely advised on the bottom at both points.

Right - A 1977-79 Monza gas tank works well, comes with electric fuel pump. 1-inch square tubing makes front mount for tank straps, filler neck is routed to fit Ford fender.

Below - Remember those 3-inch extensions on some stock chassis, this is exactly how high the Ford body is over the frame extension. If needed, mounts can be made of steel stock bent to shape.

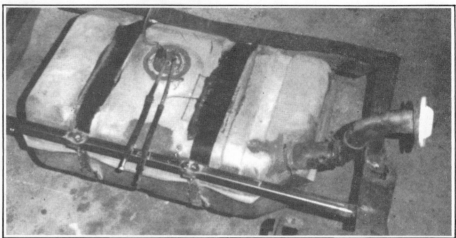

Above - New cowl mounting pads are built up to fit the particular body being used.

Above - A couple of body mounting brackets are needed at the rear, this will vary according to the body make being used.

Right - Open the inside and top flaps like this, new frame insert will slide inside the original frame. At this point, open up the original frame at rear area in same way (skip photos to see how this works) so the new frame rail insert can be jockeyed into position. Before going further, be sure the chassis is suspended at 6 points (at least) and level. Make cross and diagonal measurements of stock chassis for later reference.

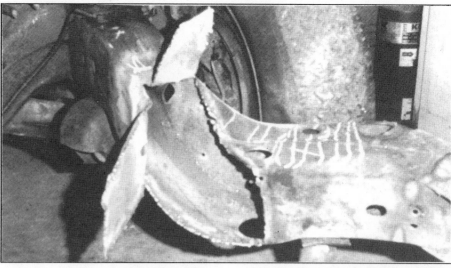

Above - Lower front ends of new frame tubes are cut to fit inside sloping stock frame, cut starts about 4 1/2 inches back, tapering to 2 1/4 width.

Above - Insert new tube in frame at rear, position in front so that tube is inside the opening. C-clamp the tube in place and form the overlapping flaps to fit inside and top of tube. (Note: Trim upper inside rear corner of new tube so it will clear indent in the stock chassis. This cut is about 2 inches long, see the later photo at this time.)

Above - With front and rear of tube inserted in stock chassis, the flaps can be welded (checking reference measurements often). The kickout portion of original frame perimeter will be cut off and discarded.

Above - Perimeter rail is cut so that there is overlap material to weld to the new tube, front and rear.

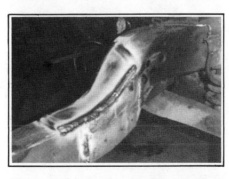

Above - Make sure that the chassis welds are excellent, your safety depends upon them.

Left - Inserted inside the stock frame at rear, the new tubing has overlaps from the original frame. These are heated and worked to fit the new tubing, held in place with be C-clamps.

Right - After measurements show everything is still straight and square, the new tube is welded in place at the rear.

Above - This is the notch cut in top inner side of frame rail before it is installed in the original frame. Cut is about 1 1/2 inches from outer side and about 1 inch deep.

Right - Here the chassis has been painted, but front of frame horns have been modified. Don't cut them until you have decided on what radiator support system you will use.

Below - Transmission mount is cut off on either end to just fit inside frame rails, this mount sits on 2x2-inch, 1/8-inch angle iron supports welded to frame rails. Bolt the tran mount in place for easier transmission service later.

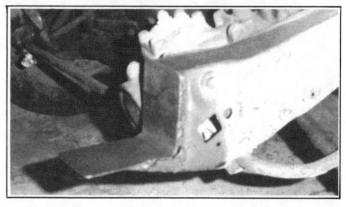

Above - If you want to use the 1965-67 GM radiator care support, cut the front horns as shown and make a mounting bracket.

Above - Perimeter rail is cut so that there is overlap material to weld to the new tube, ront and rear.

Above - Now you have a chassis that is ready for the body, modern all the way around and at a very reasonable cost.

Above - Ford convertibles have a special cowl area brace off the frame, this can be duplicated and added to the modified frame rails.

Left - Special splash aprons for inside of rear fenders should be used, make some up if you don't have them already. Relocate the gas filler neck as needed.

Right - Power brake assembly mounts to firewall with plenty of room, steering mounts at firewall slightly higher than original in order to align properly with stock GM gearbox. GM automatic transmission linkage can also be used.

Car Building Secrets Revealed!

When you are serious about the art of car building and customizing, you want to make certain that all your work is done right. So you do it yourself. You depend on your tools, and demand that they perform as promised. After all, the secret of "doing it right" is having the right tools at your disposal.

HTP America has many of the tools you need to make your projects faster and easier. Here are just a few examples:

If your projects include **welding supports in rusty frames, boxing frames, doing suspension modifications,** or any kind of bodywork, you are aware that MIG welding is the only way to go.

Our line of MIG welders is well-known for quality and versatility throughout the automotive industry.

Specifically designed for automotive welding needs, each features: a wide range of heat settings (for different thicknesses of materials); solid copper windings in transformers and choke coils; the ability to **weld steel, stainless, aluminum and cast iron without expensive add-on packages;** and accessories designed to make your automotive welding easier, such as special nozzles for welding in tight places.

Jon Kosmoski, the "King of Kustom Painting" uses our 200 amp **Maxi MIG.** You may want to choose the 170 amp **Versa MIG** or the 150 amp **Auto MIG.**

Whatever you choose, it is backed by our 2½ year warranty, and comes with a **free training video** that shows you how to make professional welds of all types.

And if you have any questions along the way, our **toll-free hotline** is there to help you out.

Planning on extensive customizing, such as top chopping? Our **Micro Cut 250 plasma cutter** will save you time and effort. Cut through sheet metal or ¼" plate with no mess and **no distortion!** There's even special cutting tips for door skins and tight corners. You'll never go back to the old ways again!

Other handy ideas?

The **Punch & Flange Tool** is the perfect way to repair patches in body panels. Use the flanging side to press a perfect flange around the perimeter of the work area. Cut a repair panel to fit this area, then punch holes along the edges of it with the punching side. Spot weld the holes, and you're ready for finishing! It also allows you to make **flush lap welds!**

HTP Heat Sponge literally **soaks up heat** from your work area when welding or brazing, to minimize distortion and discoloration of the surrounding metal. Just spread it on and go to work! (Reusable, too!)

HTP's MIG Welding Training Video is ideal for anyone who owns a MIG welder or is considering the purchase of one. This **hands-on** tape covers what to look for in a MIG, how to maintain it, troubleshoot common problems, and a **through-the-helmet-view** of the proper techniques of welding necessary for most automotive situations. This 52 minute tape contains information applicable to any brand MIG welder.

Already have a MIG welder? Chances are we have the tips, nozzles, wire and accessories you need in stock at the right price—call us to see!

Call HTP America for all your metalworking needs
1-800-USA-WELD

See us at the Nationals in Minneapolis!

HTP *America Inc.*
261 Woodwork Lane, Palatine, IL., 60067
312-934-7060 / 1-800-USA-WELD

Volare Swap

Editor's note: The Volare front end uses cross-chassis torsion bars, suspension members, and steering assembly all tied neatly to a sheetmetal K-member. This entire assembly can quite easily be adapted to virtually any car, but it is especially suitable for older customs, and any year pickup, with a ladder type frame. The only problem is track width (measurement from one tire to the other), which is wider than some earlier vehicles. However, the enterprising builder could narrow the crossmember/tie rod/and relocate the torsion bar ends on the K-member; all this to get a narrower track. We include this article on a Studebaker truck to whet your thinking cap.

by Dave McCauley

Above- The entire Volare cross-torsion bar K-member can be installed to any typical frame, by making room at the frame rails for the upper or lower A-arm. In this case, where the front end was to sit at near stock level, the top of the frame was notched for upper A-arm clearance.

Left- One of the most overlooked hot rod foundations is the Studebaker truck, this is the author's streeter after an engine swap and Volare torsion bar front suspension conversion.

Above- As originally produced, the Studebaker used a beam front axle with semi-elleptic springs and a typical ladder frame, similar to the other pickup designs.

Right- A 3-foot section of angle iron was welded to the inside and lower lip of the frame for additional strength. Length of flat stock across frame near front is just to hold rails in place temporarily.

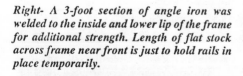

Above- This is what the Volare front K-members looks like, the torsion bars run from side to side in front of the A-arm towers and the steering gearbox tucks tightly against the left tower. The assembly can be narrowed for different track width, but this is a more difficult job than the average builder would attempt.

Left- Graphic example of why A-arm on one side must be removed from K-member tower in order to get K-member up against the frame. If the frame were narrower the unit might slip on the front. The original K-member mounting area in front (arrow) will be used with bracket off outside of frame, usually new mounting brackets must be made up.

Why in the world start with something like a Studebaker truck, when building up a streeter? The reason, in my case, is rather simple. I don't like Chevys...Everyone has a Ford...I couldn't find my first choice (Dodge)...and I just happened to find the Stude. I suspect that a very great number of street rides happen this way.

And why the Volare torsion bar front end? I noticed, while wandering around a junk yard, that the entire crossmember is held in place with just 4 bolts. Translation: That front end could be put under most anything!

When I got the Studebaker, I was going to restore it. Something I could do in a week or so, like fixing the brakes and getting the engine to run. You know the routine. But then the local parts guy said three weeks for new brake hoses. So much for restoration and patience.

Pulled the old engine, front axle, springs, etc. When I take a vehicle apart, I resort to the torch only when everything else fails. I drill out rivets, disassemble parts I won't use, and sell them to a restorer who needs the stuff (Psssst, buddy. Looking for some nice Studebaker parts?).

From a 1977 Volare wagon I removed the rear axle and springs, which bolt right to the Stude. At the front I removed the 4 main mounting bolts, disconnected the steering shaft from the gearbox, snipped the brake lines, and loosened the motor mounts. I also removed the 4 bolts that hold the upper control arm bracket, left side, to the K-member, and took off the shock. I happened to have access to a wrecker, so we lifted the car front. The K-member fell off the car when pushed to the right. Instantly, a complete torsion bar front end with steering, disc brakes, and bolt-in design. I also took the power brake booster, multi-valve, and brake pedal assembly.

If I have figured wheelbase correctly, and track width, I have something that bolts right in with no change in Ackerman, no mismatched parts, and if some parts need replacing I can get them at the parts store.

The MoPar K-member doesn't seem to have a single square surface... all curves. I flopped the unit upside down and ran a line between the lower ball joint grease fittings. From this base I found the center of the crossmember, and ran a perpendicular line to the K-member back edge. I drilled a 1/8-inch hole at the edge, for reference. This point is 8 1/8-inches from the back edge of the steering mount bracket, and 10 3/4-inches from the back edge of the idler arm

Above- New mounting brackets for the K-member, the angle iron units are for the front, the tubing/blind bolt spacers are for the rear.

Right- Gusseted angle iron brackets mount to front outside ends of the frame and extend down to original K-member mounting area, original Volare rubber insulator doughnuts have been discarded.

Above- The Volare power brake booster and dual master cylinder was mounted to Studebaker firewall, since the Volare rear end was also used, this kept entire factory brake system intact.

Above- Vega steering column is cleaner than most, here a simple mounting plate bracket comes off the top and a piece of sheet metal has been welded to the bottom collar to easy firewall mounting.

Right- Vega steering column and shaft connect to the Chrysler power gearbox via a short Borgeson splined shaft and dual U-joints, giving plenty of engine clearance and maximum steering shaft strength. Extra tubing truss above frame notch is a "just in case" addition.

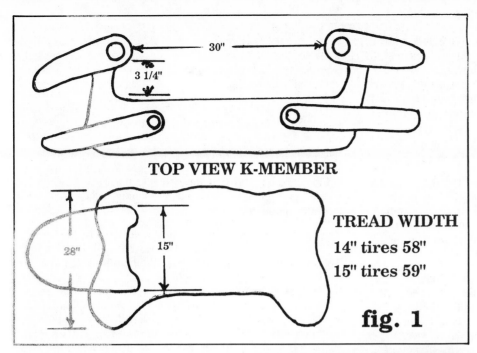

TOP VIEW K-MEMBER

30"

3 1/4"

28"

15"

TREAD WIDTH
14" tires 58"
15" tires 59"

fig. 1

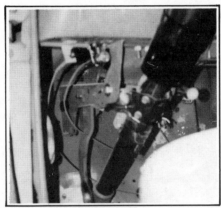

Below- Here, a frame has been notched in the bottom and the K-member inset into the notch and welded to the frame. This would lower a vehicle an additional several inches, this type of installation on pickups of the 50s and 60s will get the bumper right on the pavement. The big problem is track width, since the Volare will have a wheel track slightly wider than most older vehicles.

bracket. This assumes, of course, that all these K-members are the same on MoPars. This way I have some reference points to get the K-member square with the Stude frame. Obviously, all this will work with most any older vehicle.

The front sheet metal was removed before I took out the engine, so I could easily check to make sure the frame was both square (by measuring diagonally from known points on either frame rail) and level (with a big carpenter's level). A couple pieces of scrap metal were tack welded between the frame rails to keep them in place, and the front crossmember was removed by drilling the rivets.

Now I could check the front end for a temporary fit. The Studebaker frame is 34 inches wide, which is a benefit in that the steering box would clear, but the upper A arms would interfere. On frames that are narrower, say 28 inches, the A-arms would be no problem but there would be interference at the steering gearbox. See Figure 1. With these numbers, you can figure how the K-member will fit most any frame, and whether you will have to notch the top or bottom of the frame for clearance.

A special note when adding this type of front end to a chassis using a beam axle. As the stock beam axle goes up and down, it changes the wheelbase ever so slightly. The same thing happens with an independent front end, but when installing the independent you are probably going to have a lower spindle centerline. The common tendency is to mount the independent in such a way that the wheel center ends up slightly aft of where it should be in the fender opening. Or ahead of the centerline if you aren't careful with your measurements.

Mark the original spindle centerline on the frame before you remove the engine, etc. Or, estimate where the centerline should be, and be careful.

I decided to notch the frame top for upper A-arm clearance, because this notch would only be 16 inches long, compared to 28 inches long at the bottom. Also, a bottom notch would have lowered the front end an additional 1 3/4-inches , which was too much in the dirt for my particular needs. It does tell you how to get the front end down even lower, however.

For this frame notch, I marked off 8 inches either side of the centerline I had marked from the stock spindles. Then I came up 3 1/4-inches from the frame bottom edge and marked the lower end of the notch. I checked these soapstone lines against common reference points on the stock frame, just to make sure, then I used a centerpunch to mark the notch edges, just in case the soapstone was wiped off. This notch was cut out with a torch, A piece of 1 1/2 x 3-inch angle iron, 1/8-inch thick, was used to box the inside of the frame where it had been cut away. I installed this box plate with a series of tack welds, to keep from distorting the frame. This angle iron actually rests on the inside lower lip of the frame, and is 36 inches long. I might not have needed the extra strength, but I didn't want to take chances.

I slid the K-member under the frame and lifted it into place. Remember those 4 bolts that held the left upper A-arm in place? They turned out to be miserable to get back in. Once installed, the K-member could be squared with the frame, aligned side-to-side, leveled, and the spindle centerpoint aligned with the original centerline.

I did a final check by measuring the wheelbase...turned out to be smack on original. The K-member was then clamped to the frame with half a dozen big C-clamps. I drilled the back left side mounting hole in the frame, and installed a bolt, then measured everything. Still on. Then I drilled the opposite side, and when measuring found that I had gotten off slightly. The drill bit had grabbed an existing frame hole, with just enough force to cause misalignment, which is why there is so much measurement checking.

When I was finished, I measured top of the frame to the ground and got 22 inches, compared to the stock Studebaker number of 21 inches. I played with the torsion bar adjustment and found I had a high of 24 inches and a low of 17 inches, or a total adjustment potential of 7 inches.

The original K-member mounts via four doughnut rubber isolators. In some cases these will line up with the frame, in other cases they won't. I welded pieces of 1/8-inch stock in the oblong holes. To the K-member I welded (and bolted) some pieces of L-shape angle, and in turn bolted this L-shape bracket

to the frame. At the K-member back mounting point I used some tubing, because I wanted to increase the caster slightly over stock setting. I used castle nuts and cotter keys on these vital attachment bolts.

I like to use the Vega class steering columns. They are short (about 33 inches), have the tilt feature, mount easily with two bolts and a base collar, and if the donor car has floor shift, all that garbage is missing. In this case, I welded the collar to a piece of 16 gauge sheet stock. Be sure to remove the gasket before welding, and bolt the collar to the truck floor close to where the original fit. The Volare hanging pedals provided the steering column top mount.

The stock power steering has an output shaft of 5/8-inch OD, splined. At the Goodguys Toledo run this past year, I discovered the Borgeson booth. I told them I wanted to connect a Chrysler steering box to a Vega column. They pulled out a paper, looked it over, showed the information to me, and sent me home. I measured the shafts and counted the splines. I called Borgeson and just five days after leaving Toledo I had the parts. Just this quick editorial comment: A lot of parts suppliers should go to the Borgeson school of customer courtesy. Class folks up there.

Following the Borgeson instructions, I mounted the U-joints so that no joint angle exceeded 30 degrees (bottom joint angle is 28 degrees, top joint is 18 degrees), and before I button the project up I will put the joints in phase, although I'm not sure this is vital. All the info I can scare up says that phasing of U-joints is necessary where speed is involved. I have an '87 Dodge Dakota and those joints aren't phased.

Total cost of this swap: $100 for the 1977 Volare station wagon, $20 for the steering column, $150 for the steering U-joints, $100 to rebuild the brakes and $4.95 for some blue (hi-tek) Rust-O-Leum spray paint. Total $374.95, plus labor. I've heard of several different ways to use this front end, this just happens to be the way I did it.

Comment

The cross-chassis torsion bar arrangement used by the Volare would seem to offer some superior advantages to the custom chassis builder. And, it does. But the big stumbling block is the tread width. While the sheetmetal crossmember can easily be narrowed, the torsion bars cannot. The shorter the bars, the stiffer they become, and the only way to counteract this problem is to use either a longer actuating arm or turn down the diameter of the bar. Neither is really desirable.

Some builders of similar T-bar arrangements have found that the bars can be mounted at an angle in the chassis, but this is really going

much farther than the average builder wants.

It would seem that some kind of modification kit for the Volare bars would be an ideal thing for a parts supplier to build, probably in the form of bars that have been engineered specifically for a narrowed front end, and engineered to specific vehicle front end weights.

Of course, when a Volare front end is used, the Ackermann will be effected. As a rule, if the car is within a few inches of the Volare wheelbase. This effect will be minimal. Narrowing the front tread width also has an Ackerman effect, so keep this in mind.

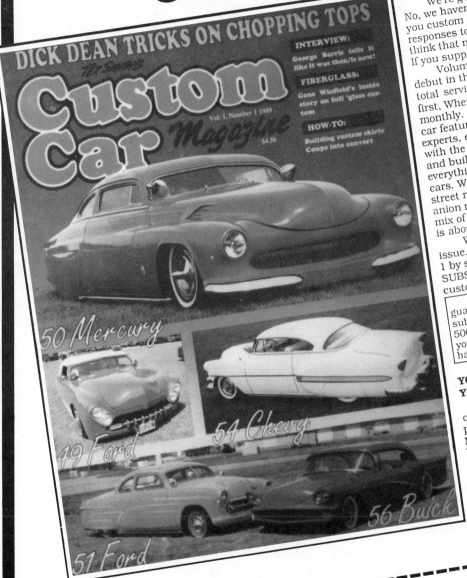

Hydraulics

Nothing looks neater than a low-down custom with barely a breath of air between bumpers and ground. But, the Earth isn't exactly a perfect surface upon which to drive such a vehicle. Speed bumps, road ruts and various obnoxious obstacles have a habit of getting in the way of a ground-hugging car.

To overcome this problem, some folks install hydraulic suspension systems that allow the car to be raised or lowered on command. Not only does this make it possible to change the ride height while driving, but it also permits the car to be lowered right to ground level after it is parked. At a car show, this is sure to inspire comments from admiring onlookers.

Installation of a hydraulic suspension system isn't extremely complicated. The components involved include hydraulic cylinders that look similar in shape and size to a shock absorber. A hydraulic pump that is powered by an electric motor, a reservoir for the hydraulic fluid, a couple of valves, a solenoid and a control unit inside the car complete the system. Hydraulic lines are routed from the pump to each of the cylinders, and when the driver toggles the control unit up or down, the pump forces the fluid through the lines either toward the cylinders or toward the reservoir to extend or retract the cylinders.

Today, hydraulics are widely used on custom cars and low-riders, and sophisticated components are readily available. But back in '64 when Bill Hines installed the first hydraulic system on a new Pontiac he was customizing, he had to hit the salvage yards to find the parts. What he came up with was a system that employed discarded aircraft components, including hydraulic pumps and cylinders that were used to raise and lower the flaps of a large airplane. Since Bill was essentially pioneering the use of hydraulics for this type of purpose, he had to design and engineer everything himself.

When we interviewed Bill at his shop (8740 Park, 2, Bellflower, California 90706; 213-634-6357) about his work in the field of hydraulic suspensions, he showed us how it all works. Of course, so much of the use of hydraulics in the low-riders today is completely different from the philosophy and physical set-up of a hydraulic system in a custom car. What we're going to touch on in this section of the book is strictly directed toward the custom crowd, not the low-riders. The differences being that the low-riders use their hydraulics to jump their cars up and down, requiring larger hydraulic cylinders, reservoirs and large banks of batteries to power the system. Custom cars use hydraulics for only one purpose and that is to allow the car to be raised high enough to be driven without damage, then lowered to the ground when it's show time.

Each application of hydraulics is going to be somewhat different, depending upon the suspension arrangement. However, the principles are the same for all cars, so you can take a look at this information and modify it in any way necessary to make it fit your particular car.

In essence, the system works like this: In order to make the car ride low, the stock suspension is altered. If coil springs are involved, it is typical to cut the spring shorter, until only about 5 coils remain. This still gives a pretty good ride, but lowers the car significantly. If leaf springs are involved, removal of leafs, installation of lowering blocks or modification of spring hanger position can be employed to bring the car down to the desired level.

Of course, all of this modification has to be calculated individually for the particular car being altered. If you want the car to be able to actually touch the ground when the hydraulics are dumped, calculate all your suspension modifications toward that goal. If you still want an inch or so of clearance, even with the hydraulics all the way down, leave enough spring under the car to keep it up that much.

When driving, it is the combination of the springs and the hydraulic cylinders that supports the car at its desired ride height. When parked at a show, and the hydraulics are dumped, the car settles and is carried only by the springs.

Typically, the front hydraulic cylinders are installed on top of and centered in the coil springs. A large cup is bolted to the end of the piston part of the cylinder, and this cup rides on the top of the coil spring. The rest of the cylinder points upward and protrudes through a hole in the upper part of the shock tower. The hole must be cut out to fit the cylinder's diameter, and is exactly where the shock absorber used to mounted. A large circular plate, called a donut, is welded to the cylinder to prevent it from moving up and down through the hole when the hydraulic system is activated.

So, the front cylinders fit between the upper part of the coil spring and the shock tower. When the system is activated, the cylinders extend, forcing the donut against the shock tower and the cup against the spring, thus raising the car. The car is always driven with the hydraulic system helping to support it's weight. It is only when parked that the system is dumped and the car lowers and is supported by the springs alone.

Setting up the rear can be a bit more complicated. If leaf springs are employed for the rear suspension system, the hydraulic cylinders must be positioned in a way that allows them to work between the axle and the body or frame. Sometimes a bracket can be attached to the body, up in the wheelwell, to serve as the upper attachment point for the cylinder. Sometimes it is necessary to build a bridge framework to run between the frame rails just below the floorpan, and have this serve as the upper support for the cylinders. Each car will be approached differently. The lower part of the cylinder can be attached to a short half/leaf that rides on top of the spring pack and protrudes just enough to support the cylinder. In operation, when the cylinders are extended, the frame (or wheelhouse brackets) and axle are forced apart by the cylinders, and the car lifts.

For the most part, salvage-yard aircraft parts are no longer available to the general public. Commonly used components today include hydraulic tailgate units that are designed for raising and lowering the tailgate of a utility truck. A southern California company named Orlie's Hydraulics (2649 Artesia Blvd., Long

Beach, California 90805; 213-634-4331) supplies the lion's share of hydraulic components to the custom and low-rider markets today.

Separate units should be installed to handle front suspension rear suspension. In other words, you need two complete tailgate systems, two reservoirs, two controls, etc. Each system will incorporate the motor, pump, check valve, dump valve, reservoir, high-pressure lines, and two hydraulic cylinders in addition to the spring-back toggle switch to control the system. A solenoid (like an automotive starter solenoid) is needed to energize the motor.

The pump must be rated for at least 600 psi, and the high- pressure lines must be rated for at least 1500 psi. Aircraft hydraulic hose is typically used. You don't want to cut corners here. Some nasty accidents have resulted from the sudden failure of a hydraulic system.

The size requirement for each reservoir depends upon the size of the cylinders used in the system. You may be using different size cylinders for the front suspension than you do for the rear, so keep that in mind. But generally a 2-quart reservoir is sufficient for each set of two of the type of cylinders that a custom car would use.

Most often, the hydraulic units are installed in the trunk. They are heavy and take up quite a bit of room. For each of the separate systems (front and rear) a main high-pressure supply hose is routed from the pump unit to the general vicinity of the hydraulic cylinders. For example, a main hose is routed forward to the engine compartment to supply the two forward cylinders. A "T" is installed, and separate hoses are run to each of the cylinders. It is vital that the length of hose running between the "T" and each cylinder is identical, in order to balance and equalize the hydraulic pressure to the cylinders. If this isn't done, one cylinder may extend and retract faster than the other.

Hooking up the electrical system and switch is fairly simple. It works a lot like a normal automotive starter. The battery is connected to the switch. One pole of the switch is connected to the solenoid, while the other is connected to the dump valve. The solenoid itself is connected to the battery and to the hydraulic pump motor. The system is grounded. That simple. Toggle the switch one way, and the hydraulic system activates to extend the cylinders. Toggle it the other way, and the dump is activated and the cylinders retract.

Frame Z'ing And C'ing

When the front or rear of the car is lowered, bringing the frame closer to the suspension/front end/rear end, expect to experience some problems in chassis component interference. Translation: The rear end hits the frame, etc. The only solution is to make more room for component travel.

Suppose you use 4-inch lowering blocks on the rear end of the car with leaf springs. This means the rear end housing is exactly 4 inches closer to the frame. It means the housing will bottom out on the Frame under most normal driving conditions. The solution is to get more clearance at the frame. By either C'ing or Z'ing the frame. Let's look at Z'ing first.

When a frame is Z'd, it is more commonly called making a "kick-up" of the frame over the rear end housing. Most late model frames already have a kick-up over the rear end. The stock frame kickup can be accentuated with a Z'ing technique that moves part of the frame even higher, just the width of the frame. This is not the same as C'ing, since it tends to retain much more of the frame strength.

The flooing in the Z'd area must be cut away and reshaped to accommodate the new frame configuration, and the driveshaft tunnel will probably need to be raised (same as with C'ing). Work on the frame for Z'ing and C'ing can be done with a torch and arc welder, it is best to have an experienced welder do all the rewelding of the frame, and add some gussets for extra strength.

Note that while these procedures are primarily intended to gain extra operating room for the front/rear ends, the rear spring shackle points can be relocated at the same time to get even more lowering. This is easier when the frame is Z'd than when it is C'd.

As a rule, hot rods use the Z'd frame more than customs, but it is often easier to Z the pre-1949 frame than to use the C'ing technique.

It must be noted that the frame extension behind the rear end must usually be returned to original position, and this is just a reversal of the Z' ahead of the axle.

With the profile of the stock frame drawn on the garage floor, it is an easy matter to calculate and draw the modifications on the cement to make a pattern. This helps prevent errors in frame modification.

To Z the frame using method B, pie-shaped pieces of frame must be removed to create the new angle. Before cutting, mark with chalk or scribe on the frame the area to be removed.

Using a torch or other cutting tool, remove the pie-shaped wedge from the frame.

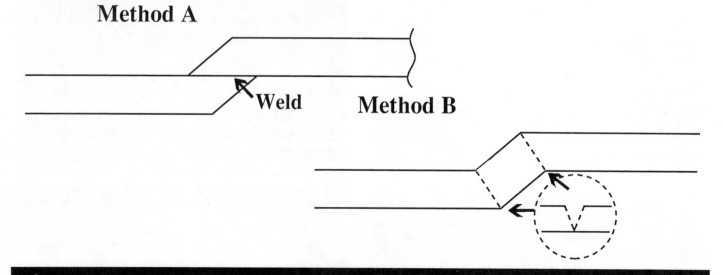

Left - Clean up the cut with a grinder so that the welding job will be cleaner and more solid.

Above - On this frame, the lower cut has already been welded, while the upper cut is still open to illustrate how this modification works.

Method A

Weld

Method B

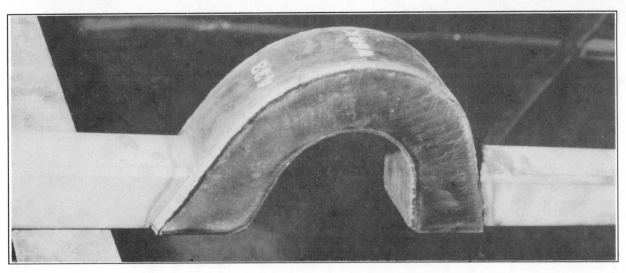

The practice of C-ing a frame is mostly done when trying to lower a custom car, but it does come into play with rod building. Here the entire C-section has been constructed of plate stock, then the C is inserted in frame tubing.

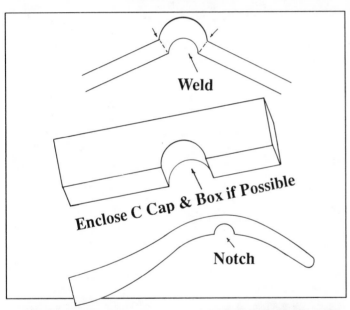

Weld

Enclose C Cap & Box if Possible

Notch

Frame C-ing is much more popular on custom cars, since such customs are almost always made from 1949 and newer marques. Here, the body is seldom removed from the frame, and only a small amount of extra clearance is needed above the rear axle.

Whether Z'ing or C'ing a frame, it is wise to place some kind of limit bumper between the frame and the rear end housing. While this reduces the amount of extra travel available, it often keeps a rear end housing from being damaged. It definitely saves on occupant nerves when driving over a bad road.

If the frame area above the rear end is around 6 inches in width (top to bottom), it is possible to C the area almost 4 inches. Just keep in mind that a very large amount of strength can be lost at the point of the C unless it is boxed. In some cases, it may even be necessary to add some metal above the cutaway section. Use heavy plate for the C section and for boxing, something on the order of 1/8 or 3/16 inch. This is no place to skimp. Arc welds will work as well as more exotic TIG or MIG welds, do not grind away all the strength of the welds just for the sake of cosmetics.

With either a Z or C section to the frame, it will probably be necessary to reshape the flooring. Usually, nothing more than additional driveshaft tunnel room and some room over the rear end center section is needed. Sometimes, however, it will require a complete rework of the entire flooring above the rear end. Nothing really unique or difficult here, except for the problems of removing body underseal prior to welding.

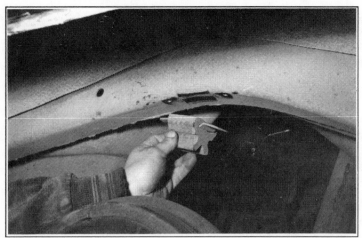

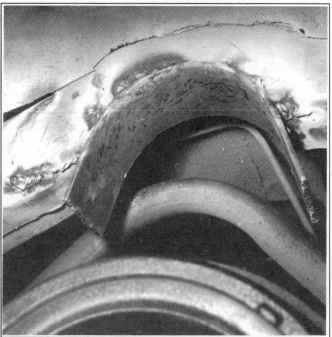

The object is to provide more clearance between axle housing and frame. Start by removing the stock bump stop.

Above - Although the work has not yet been finished, this photo shows how the C is cut into the frame rail and sealed by welding plate stock across the opening.

Below - When suspension and frame modifications are made, it is often necessary to remove portions of the frame to provide adequate clearance.

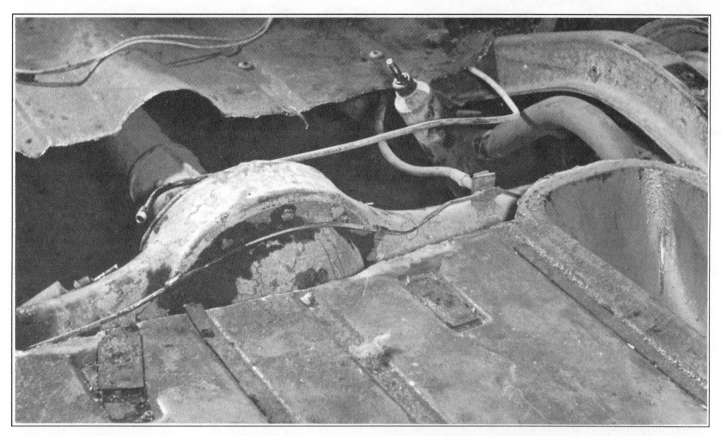

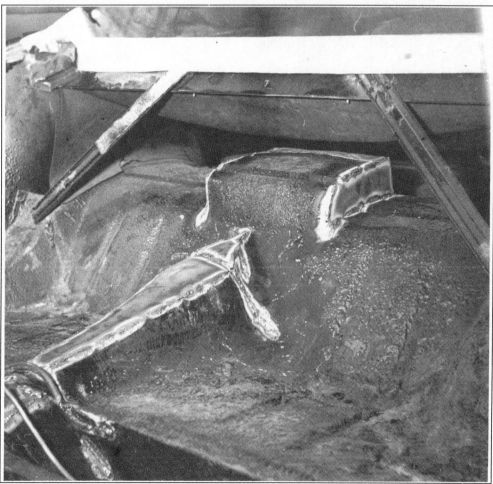

Above - Z'ing or C'ing the frame essentially lowers the floorpan in relation to the axle housing. This makes it necessary to modify the floor to allow clearance as the axle housing moves up and down on the suspension. Here, a section of the floor has been cut away in preparation for the final modification work.

Right - The driveline tunnel and a section of the floor above the differential housing have been raised to provide clearance. Sometimes, it is necessary to perform even more radical floor modifications, depending upon the particular car and the amount of Z'ing or C'ing that has been done to the frame.

POWER

by Robert Hardy

When building a custom car, the engine choice and state of tune must satisfy three requirements; 1, be reliable, 2, move this piece of automotive art at a pace actually described as "ain't no slouch", and 3, look good. I fully realize that several pro/street style sleds have been built and many more are likely to be coming forth, but this is a small segment of our hobby and their particular engine interests are better served in publications other than this book.

Reliability is most important, "kustoms are for kroozin' and stranded ain't kool". A stock engine is about as reliable as you can get, but there are some modifications that can be done that will change that engine into something that is much more suitable for what we have in mind. We can improve performance in the low to mid r.p.m. range, make it look much better and possibly even increase its fuel mileage. This is all relatively simple to do, and you don't have to be an engine building expert to make one dynamite looking and performing engine.

ENGINE CHOICE

Probably the most commonly chosen engine to power a custom car is one of the many variations of small blocks produced by Chevrolet and Ford. So these are what we'll look at first.

SMALL BLOCK CHEVROLET

The Chevy small block has been produced in ten different cubic inch sizes over the years (can you name them?), but four of these displacements have proven to be the most popular. The 350 inch engine is the most favored because, it is still being produced so parts are readily available, and it is a good sized motor with enough available power to satisfy most people but still will give respectable fuel mileage and is dead reliable. The 283-327 Chevys are still preferred by many, but these engine sizes have not been produced for quite a number of years and although aftermarket rebuild parts are readily available, good rebuildable cores at decent prices are getting harder to come by. In fact, I have seen many 283-327's priced higher than a 350 Chev in comparable condition. For this reason alone a 350 usually becomes the GM engine of choice, unless you have a soft spot in your heart for the earlier engines or can get a good deal on one. I believe the late model 305 c.i. engine will be used more and more as time goes on. GM has really emphasized this particular motor and although not a personal favorite, it should become a solid engine choice simply because of the numbers in which it is being produced.

BIG BLOCK CHEVROLET

The big block Chevy is one of those engines that like the 427 Ford and the Chrysler Hemi, made it big during the muscle car years and has since developed an aura about itelf. This is good because of the usual ooh's and ahh's when you open the hood, but it's bad because it raises the price of anything associated with these engines. Any of the car and light truck versions of this engine are fine to use. Stay away from the heavy duty truck engines, for even if they may be of the same cubic inch size as a car engine, it's not even the same block. If you must run a Chevrolet and need more low r.p.m. torque than you can get with any small block then by all means use a big block, but be aware of the added expense and larger physical size. As with the small block Chevy there is a tremendous amount of aftermarket equipment available for these engines.

SMALL BLOCK FORD

The three most popular Ford small blocks are the 302w (Windsor), the 351w, and the 351C (Cleveland). The Cleveland is for those horsepower freaks in the crowd who for one reason or another don't want to move up to a big block. Many aftermarket items are available for this engine and it would make an excellent choice for a custom except for two minor flaws. It has large horsepower producing cylinder head ports that give away some low r.p.m. torque and mileage in exchange for top end power. It is also physically larger than the Windsor series and that may make it more difficult to install in some cars. Even with these slight faults it is still a good choice. The 351w and its slightly smaller brother, the 302w, not only drop into a chassis easier than a Cleveland but the performance difference on the street is small. The Windsor is not too shabby in the power department, witness the late model 302 Mustang.

BIG BLOCK FORD

Ford has made many big block engines over the years, many of them very good engines, but I believe that the 429-460 engine makes the better choice. The FE series (390-427 etc.) was THE Ford big block for many years, but many of these engines are getting pricey, and it is a design born in the fifties. The 429-460 is a late model engine still in production. Performance parts are readily available and it takes tons of torque, plus, many can still be picked up quite cheaply. This motor looks and almost acts like a Cleveland on sterioids. This engine would be harder than a small block to fit into many cars and the mileage would be a little less, but even in stock configuration it would have enough power to satisfy most people and if you have to pull a trailer, this is the best Ford engine you could pick.

One item that may cause difficulty when installing a Ford engine into a non-original chassis is the oil pan. Most of these engines have a front sump which can get into the way of the front chassis cross-member and/or steering linkage. This problem can be avoided by switching to a rear sump oil pan and oil pump pick-up, which are available from Ford and afterrmarket suppliers for some Ford engines.

NOSTALGIA ENGINES

Now for all you nostalgia buffs who patiently waded through all that late model stuff, here's something for you. The Ford flathead and early GM inlines never really disappeared, there have always been a few "fanatics" around to proclaim their merits, But their popularity have had a big resurgence within the last few years, and besides, there is nothing like a nostalgia engine to compliment a nostalgia custom. If you are planning to use one of these engines you must realize and be prepared for their shortcomings. Parts and rebuildable engines can be hard to come by. This may prove disastrous if it breaks down on the road many miles from home. For this reason it is wise to carry some spare parts with you, such as some ignition, fuel and cooling system parts, when you venture from home. Not a bad idea for any vehicle really. Also, these engines put out less horsepower than late model powerplants, but I have to admit they've got a lot of grunt down low that can easily make up for their lack of top end power. Besides, I don't think that there are too many of us old-timers (that's baby boomers to you youngins, gad how time flies) who don't have a soft spot in their hearts for these engines.

FLATHEAD FORD

The flatheads have really made a comeback recently, with speed equipment and information being offered by many of the reputable aftermarket suppliers. A number of different models of this historic engine were offered by Ford between 1932 and '53. The better flatmotors, for our purposes, were produced after WWII (world war two). The 1946-48 engine has the bellhousing cast as part of the block, with the oil pan also forming the lower flywheel cover portion of the housing. The upper radiator hoses attach to the upper center of each cylinder head, and the distributor is driven directly by the cam and is mounted on the timing cover. I believe Offenhauser still makes an adapter to mate a Muncie four speed to this engine, but, it's that integral bellhousing that makes this engine difficult to use. The stock trannys weren't very strong to start with and a modified engine just puts added strain on a forty plus year old part. So, you can't reliably use a stock transmission and late model transmissions (with that one exception) won't adapt, and automatics are out of the question.

The 1949-53 flathead is a better choice. It has a detachable bellhousing and adapters are available to bolt up late model four speeds and the Ford C-4 automatic. In fact, with the right bits, a Ford top-loader bolts right up. This later flatty can also be identified by the distributor being mounted at the upper front of the block, and the water outlets mounted at the front of the cylinder heads. A separate bellhousing makes this the better flathead to use.

EARLY GM INLINES

These early inline six cylinders have always had a small steadfast following, but over the last several years the "six in a row for show and go" group has become quite a going concern. If you have ever heard a big six with a split manifold laying down some serious power and sounding for all the world like a WWII bomber straining for take-off, or felt the gut wrenching torque these babies can produce, then you'll know why more and more people are being turned on to these inlines.

Both the Chevy and GMC versions have so many basic similarities that we'll consider them together. From 1937 to 1952 the standard Chevy engine was a 216 cubic inch beast with a combination pressure/splash oil system. In 1953 they started using a full pressure lubrication system and these later engines would make a better choice for any road going car strictly for the added reliability insurance a full pressure system offers. These later engines, depending on whether it's a Chevy or a GMC, range in size from 235-302 c.i. One of these big sixes, equipped with some mild performance equipment (many of which can be found in the pages of Hot Rod Mechanix) will make for a surprising performer, even in a heavier custom. As a further testament to this engine's popularity, there are supercharger kits and automatic transmission adapters now on the market for these inlines. One other factor to consider, many of the General Motors vehicles were built to accept this engine or other inlines making this engine very easy to use in many cases. If a V8 was to be used in these cars, many times the steering box becomes an interference point and may have to be moved. This can make it tough if you are long on enthusiasm but short on tools and money.

POWER PARTS

We're going to take a quick overview of performance equipment keeping one thing in mind, this is a street engine. A good streetable engine will have three main factors going for it; 1, reliability, 2, good power production from idle to about 3500 r.p.m., which is where most driving is done, and 3, decent fuel mileage. All the items here will stress these three points just as you should as you build up your engine.

Probably the first item to be changed on an engine, besides the usual dress-up stuff, is the carburetor and intake manifold. A good street combination is a small four barrel carb with vacuum secondaries and a matching intake manifold that works particularly well in the lower r.p.m. ranges. Manifolds and carbs that fill this bill are currently available for all the engines that have been discussed. Now, there are those of you that will want the look of multiple carbs, either 3 X 2 bbls or possibly 2 X 4 bbls. This look was very much a part of the past and it is coming back as with most other nostalgia items. The multiple carb systems that always looked so wild are now being produced again for many engines. The 3 X 2 setup is probably the most streetable of all the multiple carb systems available. When properly adjusted the engine does all its running on the center two barrel, and then as the accelerator pedal demands more power the other two carbs come into the act. This provides good mileage, with the extra power when you want it. Other multicarb systems are available but consult with the manufacturer for installation and tuning procedures, and to make sure that it will work well in your particular situation. Please, don't forget, no open velocity stacks, there are plenty of attractive air filter housings on the market so there is absolutely no reason for letting dirt into that fresh rebuild that you spent so much time and money on.

Still staying on the outside of the engine, the next item most people think about is headers. Tubular steel headers do increase performance and can even help fuel mileage under certain circumstances, but they can be difficult to install, are noisier, prone to leaks and require constant maintenance. If you are willing to put up with this, and can find a set to fit your car/engine combination, then go ahead, but buy a quality set. It's just too much work to replace a set of headers that didn't last or to be continually chasing leaks. A quality set of headers will eliminate most of this. Another type of exhaust manifold making a comeback is the cast iron header. This is now available for the Ford flathead, early GM inline sixes and of course the ever popular small block Chevrolet. This header provides a power increase close to that of the more common tubular steel units but has the sound deading qualities, life expectancy, and low maintenance factors of stock manifolds. Speaking of stock manifolds, it is perfectly all right to use them if all out performance is not one of your goals, and if an engine swap doesn't make it necessary to use headers to solve some clearance problem. The thing that bothers most people about stock manifolds is that they don't look very nice. This can easily be solved by making up some polished stainless steel covers for them. These covers are even available through aftermarket sources for the more popular engines. For the rest of the exhaust system you don't have to get fancy, just don't make it restrictive. A dual exhaust system, a classic in itself, with a set of free-flowing turbo type mufflers would fill the bill nicely.

For the sake of reliability it would be wise, although not necessary, to change from the old point/condenser style ignition to electronic. Drop-in factory electronic ignitions for all the popular engines discussed as well as many aftermarket systems as well. The nostalgia guys will have it a little harder, but it shouldn't be to difficult to put an electronic kit into the original distributor housing. The only distributor that this would probably not work on is the 49-53 Ford flathead, this is a vacuum advance only model and is worthless even on a stock engine. Fortunately Mallory still makes a good dual-point unit that could be converted to electronic if your wished. Electronic ignitions have several points (no pun intended) that place them head and shoulders above mechanical distributors; almost no maintenance, higher secondary voltages available at the spark plug for starting as well as running, larger plug gaps can be used which leads to superior combustion, the spark plugs last longer and more, but you get the idea.

If you're still looking for more performance then the only way to go is to get inside the engine. After improving the intake and exhaust systems the limiting factor becomes the camshaft. Stock cams are one big compromise. The manufacturer doesn't know what you are going to do with the engine (strictly around town, pulling a trailer etc.), where you are going to live (at sea level or 4000 feet), and a multitude of other questions. So they design a cam that will cover all applications fairly well and provide acceptable fuel mileage as well. The best way to buy a camshaft is to contact a reputable cam grinder and ask them to suggest a cam for your particular application. Who better to know what cam to pick than the guys that designed them? Be prepared to answer a lot of specific questions about your engine, car, and its intended use. These guys are thorough. If you must pick out a cam on your own, choose one that works best in the idle to 3500 r.p.m. range. In reality, this is where most street driving is done.

OK, are you ready for the part that draws everybody's attention when you open the hood and will make you king of the drive-in? Well, I'm not going to tell you what to do. Wait! Don't go away mad.

Engine accessories and dress-up items can really highlight a good running engine and make it look like a real showpiece. But there are so many custom parts to stick under a hood, that together they would sink a battleship. The number of pieces available is so staggering that I'm going to leave it up to you to pick and choose the items that best fit your car and pocketbook.

Remember, keep it streetable. Refer to those three requirements in the opening paragraph. It's not hard to build an engine affordably that will last for many years, if you keep it simple. You may have noticed that no mention was made of, forged pistons, steel crankshafts, porting and polishing etc., they're simply not needed. If by chance, you are faced with a total engine rebuild, a balance job would be a good idea as the factory uses some pretty wide tolerances, but even this is not necessary. Besides, if you don't have to put a lot of time into modifying and blueprinting your engine, you can spend more time doing body mods, or better yet, CRUSIN'!

EXHAUST

Photos by John Lee

Above Right - For his '54 Chevy sedan delivery, Roger Ward made exhaust tips out of 1 1/2" x 3" rectangular tubing and cut slight notches in the bumper to fit them up tight.

Right - Exhaust tips on Ed Guffey's '50 Ford protrude through openings cut into the bumper insert and molded with 1/4" round rod.

by C.J. Brockman
Brockman Mellowtones

Remember when a Ford sounded like a Ford and a Chevy sounded like a Chevy. Things have come full circle. You can get the sound again.

For years, I looked for mufflers that would give that sound, but everything I found sounded like corn popping. Finally, I decided to make my own mufflers. I started with a heavy 16-gauge steel for the body, so the sound wouldn't escape through the 3-inch casing. Through trial and error I developed the core, also out of 16-gauge, but with a twist that "Chubby" would be proud of.

The packing I use in the glass packs has a melt point of 1250 degrees, so that they don't burn out like the old ones did. The steel packs are constructed with heavy steel strand. The glass packs have a very deep and mellow sound, as do the steel packs, but the steel packs are a little louder (just like the old steel packs).

Brockman mufflers are not mass produced, they are handmade one at a time. For the majority of cars, either the 24-inch or the 30-inch muffler is perfect. Some MoPars need a 30-36-inch unit to get the same deep and mellow tone. The longer the muffler, the quieter the car, but still with the deep tone.

For the best sound, install the muffler from the car's midpoint forward. The longer the tailpipe, the better the sound. For big block and high performance engines above 300 hp, I recommend a muffler with either a 2 1/4 or 2 1/2-inch core. This reduces back pressure.

Remember the sound you used to get when the car was back into the garage, or parked under an overpass? All from those driveshafts you cut for echo cans? I recommend at least a 12-inch can, if you have room the 18-inch long echo can sounds even better, diameter is 3 or 3 1/2 inch size.

Housings made out of larger diameter tubing have been decorated with diagonal cut-out slots and welded to the fender and rocker panels for frenched lakes pipe styling.

Right - Jerry Johnson uses 3" echo cans under the rolled pan on his '54 Olds 88.

Below - Chromed gear cogs were slipped over the lakes pipes to provide extra decoration on this custom.

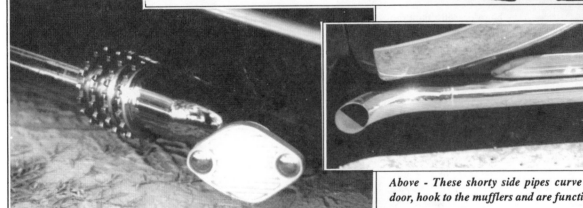

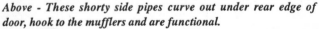

Above - These shorty side pipes curve out under rear edge of door, hook to the mufflers and are functional.

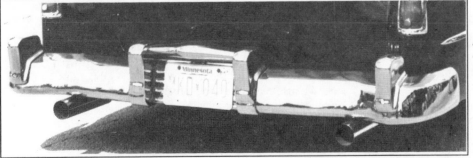

Left - Straight tips like the chrome 3" echo cans on this '51 Chrysler are a popular choice.

Flamethrowers

Yes, it is possible to make flamethrowers for the custom exhaust, but we strongly advise against them. They can be, and are, dangerous. They were long ago, and they are now, especially when someone decides to add propane to the system.

The flamethrower is made by putting a spark plug in the exhaust tip, and firing this plug via a coil (such as Model T) and switch. Rev up the engine (or pull out the choke), let off on the gas to get an overly rich fuel mixture into the exhaust, and light the plug. Some events encourage these contests, just be aware that they can catch clothing and other vehicles on fire. Flamethrowers were used on specialty cars long before the custom scene started, and they are against the law in many states. Be forewarned.

An Exhausting Primer

Form and function travel together when it comes to an exhaust system. Even though only the tip of the exhaust system may be visible, there is a lot of unseen work that needs to go into a great custom exhaust system. If the work is done right, it can make all the difference.

By David Lord

Down thru the years there have been literally hundreds of articles on exhaust systems. There really is only one type of exhaust system for the internal combustion engine. How it is designed and assembled is another topic that could fill an entire book.

The first thing to do when you set out to build an exhaust system for your custom is to get the car up on stands and look the entire chassis over. Be sure and use good quality jack stands and never support the car with a floor jack or bumper jack because you will be moving around under the car a lot. Now, look for obstacles. The things that make street rod exhaust systems complicated are normally not found in cars built after 1950. Cars of this era usually have a very heavy x-member with holes on each side that match. On a low riding custom, the exhaust system must go through these holes in the frame in order to gain ground clearance.

Chevrolets from 1955-up (and most other GM products except converts had wide box frames and flat floor pans that made exhaust systems easy to build.

Now comes the time to start your shopping list. The type of manifolding on your engine dictates what size of tubing you will use. After you have settled on the size, calculate the length. Start at the manifold or header, and bend the tape measure around to roughout the bends. A good rule of thumb is to add one foot per pipe to be safe. Now, go down to your local muffler shop and buy a handful 45"'s and 90"'s and maybe a joint or two of pipe. This will be your pattern material. It would be a lot easier to have a shop bend a system for your car, but most shops either can not or will not take the time to build the system where it looks, fits and performs as it should.

Cut the elbows and tubing and tack weld them together until you get back to the point where your muffler will join. Look for places to mount hangers that will be both heavy enough to support the system, yet flexible enough to let the system expand and contract and not hit anything. Generally 2 inches between frame and floor pans, and at least 6 inches clearance between the bottom of the tailpipe and the top of the rear-end housing will keep you out of trouble. Remember to keep it neat, simple, and above all functional. These are just the basics. We'll start with the tricks now.

Manifolds

Stock manifolds leave little to be desired in the department of looks and even less in performance. With the exception of certain rare hi-po manifolds, most are low performers and have no place on a high performance engine. If you want to keep manifolds on your engine, but want a little better breathing out of them, you can port match them to the heads and use bigger tubing. One neat trick is to remove the studs from the manifold and weld the tubing to the flange, then attach it to the manifold using the header bolts. If for example, you're using stock 350 c.i. chevy truck manifolds ('69-'72) you can go from the stock 2 1/2 inch tubing all the way up to 2-inch tubing just by turning out the inside of the flange to match the o.d. of your tubing. You would be surprised at how good this looks and works.

Balance Pipes

There has been a lot of discussion about balance tubes. A lot of people will say they increase low-end torque, while still others say they only decrease noise level. If everything is adjusted properly, a balance tube will provide a minimal increase on low-end torque, with a reduction in noise. For best results, the balance tube should be installed 18 to 24 inches from the headers. Find a point where the pipes are parallel and measure from center to center of the pipes. If that measurement is 24 inches, use a pipe 26 inches long. Now measure the distance between the two pipes. This measurement is 22 inches. Draw a line 2 inches from the end of the pipe on each end. Using a cut off saw, cut a 45" on each side of the pipe using the seam as a guide on both ends, file the edges off, slip it in and mark all the way around it. Remove the pipe and cut out the center. Now slip the pipe back in and your ready to weld. Nothing to it, Right?

Flanges, Clamps, Etc.

When it comes time to put all this stuff together, there are numerous ways you can attack it. Welding is good if you never intend to take it apart. Clamping is easier to install, but still not easy to remove when you have to. Flanges are the best of both worlds. You can remove the entire system, or just one part in minutes by just removing the bolts and gaskets. It is more time consuming to build, but the time that it will save you later on more than offsets the labor involved initially.

Coatings & Maintenance

You can build your system out of steel and have it aluminized, plated, or H. P. C. coated. This provides a durable finish that requires a minimum of maintenance. A system built out of aluminized steel tubing is better (lasts 3-5 times longer than steel tubing) and requires no maintenance. Stainless steel is the best of all worlds, but may be beyond the price range of some builders. Whichever material you use, you can get show-car looks and hot :rod performance if you are patient and look at each piece as part of an integrated system.

Mufflers

With thousands of mufflers to pick from, it can get confusing as to what to put on your pride and joy. This is where it will get confusing. Turbo mufflers provide a good balance between back-pressure and sound. Currently the best turbo-muffler is the Super Turbo manufactured by WALKER. This muffler features full size tubing throughout the muffler with curved exhaust deflectors in the end caps. This results in a very free flowing muffler with good noise control. Stock mufflers take up a lot of room and with very few exceptions, don't flow very well. The time honored glass pack will always be popular because of its compact size and low price.

Tricks & Tips

To help make removing your headers or manifolds easier, coat all belts and studs with anti-seize compound. When using stainless bolts and nuts, coat the threads liberally with the compound to prevent galling. To help prevent header leaks, soak the gaskets in water for about 45 minutes. After you install the gaskets, crank the car and allow it to run for 5 minutes. Then retorque all bolts. No more leaks or lost bolts.

Summary

While there is no substitute for experience, if you use careful planning and the proper materials and tools, you can build an exhaust system that looks and works as good as those built by a professional.

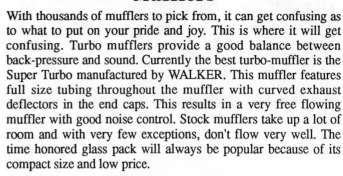

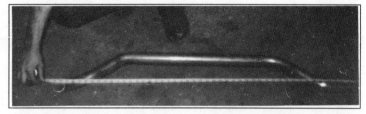

Above Left - After the measurements are determined, bend the tubing to clear any obstacles under the car. Be careful to maintain proper clearances between floor pan, frame rails & suspension components.

Above Right - Measure tubing to get the total length needed. Remember to add at least 1 ft. per pipe to allow for shortening caused by bending.

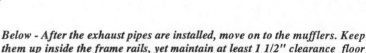

Below - After the exhaust pipes are installed, move on to the mufflers. Keep them up inside the frame rails, yet maintain at least 1 1/2" clearance floor & muffler.

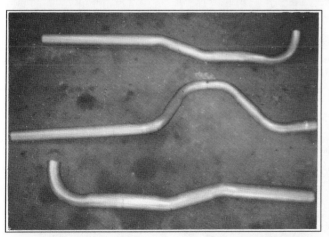

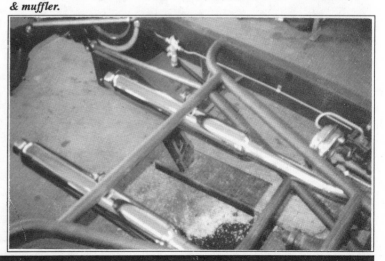

Above - Be sure to keep both sides as close as possible to a perfect match. Remember, you want one side to look like a reflection of the opposite.

BODY

Other than the grille, one of the most important custom design elements is the side trim. While many customs are designed and built sans any kind of trim, others utilize trim pirated from a different car for unusual design statements.

While this trim may be a part of the overall design, it also serves to protect the door and side panels from the parking lot wars, where the doorslammers eat everything in sight.

As a general rule, when selecting a different car's trim, you try to get pieces that fit exactly at the door opening, or are slightly larger. While it is possible to cut and weld trim to make a longer piece, this is difficult at best. Much of the trim on cars of the earlier years will be of stainless, but some is plated steel. The stainless is best, but anything can be used.

Finally, some customizers have even gone to the trouble of finding shaped solid metal stock and built it up for chroming. Here, we show you how trim is cut and fit to work, and we close some ideas of trim use. From here on, it's up to you.

Cutting Chrome

by Cris Boggess

You know the story. You wander around a rod and custom event and you see all the trick and keen chrome trim that is used on the customs (and sometimes the restorations), and you must know it isn't stock. Or, if it is stock, it just seems to be slightly different somehow. You ask the owner, and he says, "Oh, I just took something off a such and such car and shortened it to fit." Like maybe this is something we all do everyday. Yeah, sure Gene Autry.

Fortunately, it isn't difficult to shorten or modify chrome or stainless trim. In the case I show here, the owner wanted to shorten the chrome strip on the rear quarters of his 1950 Mercury 4-door. That is these strips could then be used on the doors for a shorter strip, getting rid of the Mercury emblem (front fender). Follow along.

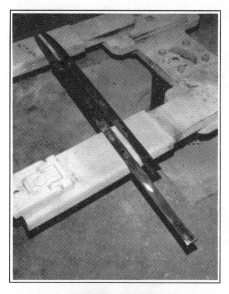

You start off by not doing anything! To the piece you are going to use, that is. Start by cutting off the strip you will use, but cut it a bit longer than what you really want. This is so you can do some practice bending of the cut-off end. What we are doing here applies to just about any trim piece.

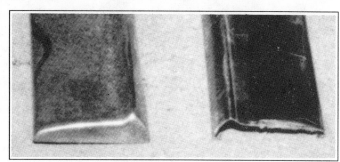

This is the end of a trim piece that has been cut, you can use a hacksaw or, (very carefully) snips. This leaves and open end that must be "boxed".

Using the piece you cut off (the piece you will likely discard), practice making an end box. Using tin snips (sharp ones!), cut a small V-shape where the trim rolls or folds at an angle.

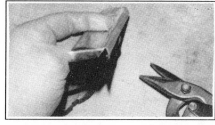

Now very carefully fold one piece over at a 90-degree angle. It is important to get pliers, and you may use a hammer and tight angle dolly.

Trim the folded over edges to look like the original end, you may want to do a super finish with a hand file on the cut edges.

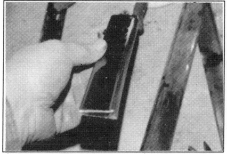

Next, roll the remaining edge over at the same 90-degree angle. It is important to get a good crease at the roll, but not damage the trim that is visible.

Right - We are still working with the practice piece of trim here. Try this on the door to see that it fits just right, and now you know exactly how much to trim the real piece, and how to make the bends.

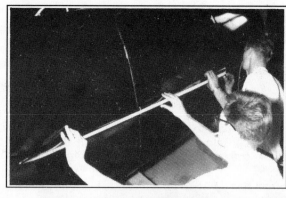

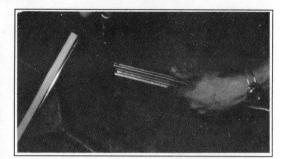

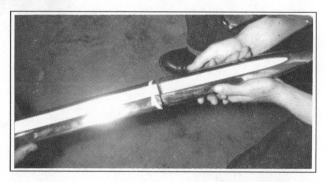

Photos by Gene Winfield

Creating a great looking spear for the side of this shoebox Ford involved several steps, but was not particularly difficult. Start with a suitable, but too long, spear that has been salvaged from another car. Holding the trim up against the car in the exact location where the piece will eventually fit, mark with masking tape where the cuts will need to be made. Then, employing a hacksaw, carefully sever the trim in the appropriate spot. You might want to cut the piece a little long so you can work it down to the exact length during the finishing process. Better too long than too short at this point. Using snips, a grinder wheel and flat file, the finished shape and length of the trim piece is achieved.

If a vise is used to hold the trim while filing the ends, wrap cloth around it to prevent damage. As the finish work is being done, check and recheck to ensure a square fit where the trim is broken at the edges of the door and the fender. When the pieces are installed, make sure there is enough separation where the door opens to prevent the trim pieces from hitting each other. Some hinges allow the gap to widen as the door opens, but others can pinch the trim pieces together and cause damage.

Changing Trim

by Cris Boggess

Along with other custom tricks, Party Doll receives a new side trim treatment. After the stock trim is removed, a piece is selected that sweeps from just above the front wheel openings to the point where scoops will be built in the rear fenders. Preliminary fitting is done with masking tape to hold the trim in the general vicinity of the final installation positon.

The general angle of the trim on the door is established and the piece is held in place with masking tape. It isn't taped too securely at this point because it may be necessary to change the angle of the trim a bit.

Notice that more masking tape has been added to hold the trim once the exact position has been decided. Another strip of tape is laid across the trim where it will be cut for the door opening.

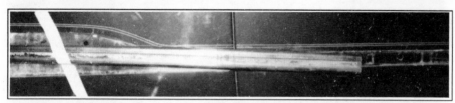

The piece of trim on the fender must align precisely with the angle of the door trim. Use scribe marks on the door and fender to mark the exact position of the two pieces.

Once the fender trim angle has been established, double up on the tape and mark with another strip of masking tape where the piece needs to be cut.

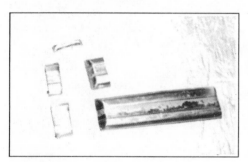

Below - After cutting both pieces, they are aligned and again taped in place with the appropriate gap at the door opening.

Right - If you look close, you can see the scribe marks along the side of the car to indicate the exact position of the trim pieces. It is critical to have a smooth flowing trim line from one end to the other.

Later on in the customizing process, after Party Doll had received her rear fender scoops, the side trim was taped in place for final adjustment before installation. This particular application leads the eye in one smooth motion from the front wheels to the rear scoops. With a pencil, both edges of the trim were outlined on the side of the car to make it easy to position trim clips.

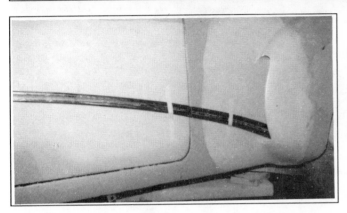

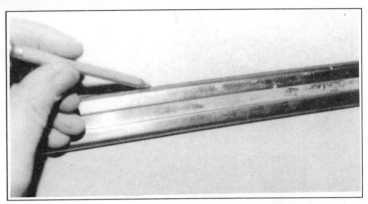

Trim Examples

by John Lee

Right -Spear-shaped trim was a Packard trademark for several years. These strips on Jim Stockton's '49 Chevy custom are from a '51 or '52.

Left - Sweep spears on '54 (shown) through '56 Buicks are a neat design for swapping to other cars, especially with radiused rear wheel openings.

Gary Sams' '56 Canadian Meteor came with a radical set of stainless side trim, completely different from U.S. Ford.

Left - 55 DeSoto trim was a custom favorite in the '50s, especially adaptable to two-toning. DeSoto had similar versions through '57.

Below - Trim on this '56 Buick appears to be '55 Pontiac inverted, although '54 Olds is similar. Pods have been molded to the fender skirt to french in long lakes pipes on this '56 Buick.

In a previous incarnation, Jimmy Vaughn's '51 Chevy used the front portion of '54-56 Buick trim to divide two-tone paint. Note how the trim shape follows the fastback roof line.

A sweep similar to '52-53 Buick in a slimmer spear is offered by the '59 Pontiac trim, shown here on a '50 Ford.

'58 Ford Fairlane 500 trim with its gold anodized insert is installed here on a '56 Chevy, which also has a '57 Buick back window added to the chopped roof.

'55 Pontiac trim gives a very clean look and is ideal for two-toning like on Gary Howard's '52 Ford.

When Ford brought out the Crestliner trim in '51, lots of owners added it to their '49, '50 and '51 models, but it's a hard set to find these days.

Above - '56 Dodge spear has a nice sweep to it, but we don't recall seeing a custom application of it.

Right - Wide, curved '52-'53 Buick sash has never been used better than on Jack Walker's '51 Merc. It exactly follows the window line.

Below - '57 Plymouth Savoy has a clean trim treatment that could adapt well to other cars.

Bottom - A '57 Chevy rear fender strip was added to this '51 Ford to provide a subtle two-tone accent.

Polishing

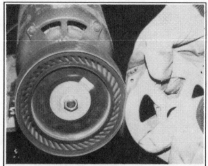

Far Left - Buffing project begins with removing alternator. Follow your shop manual for dissembly instructions. Save all parts.

Left - Start by polishing (sanding) the rough, cast finish, using Eastwood's #1809 Expander Wheel, 1800 rpm motor.

Courtesy the Eastwood Company

There is a great deal that the home craftsman can do the brightwork of his custom, which saves a bundle of money in the long run, and adds considerably to the sense of accomplishment. Buffing aluminum and stainless parts is one prime example, something that can be done with a minimal of equipment and working space.

There are a number of suppliers of buffing supplies and equipment advertising in rod and restoration publications, one of the best known suppliers is the Eastwood Company, call toll free 1-800-345-1178 for a free catalog (foreign call 1-215-640-1450). Eastwood publishes a special Auto Restoration News supplement, and graciously permitted us to reproduce their guide to buffing an aluminum alternator housing. Stainless buffing (side trim, etc is very similar, although wheel grits and rouge may differ. The point is, here is something that anyone can do, and it makes a powerful difference in detailing appearance.

In just seconds, the first pass on the expander wheel produces very noticeable results, Note the contrast. Simply work around the piece

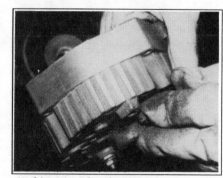

Continue working evenly all around the alternator housing. Grip the part firmly and wear gloves since the parts get hot.

Note how the flexible expander wheel can fit around projections and odd shaped areas of the housing. Try to smooth as much as possible.

At this point, the alternator has been polished with 120 grit. The belt is changed to the next finer grit, 220.

Continue to use expander wheel's flexibility to get into tight spots, Here we're working around a bolt boss.

The rear of the alternator shows in most installations. We're smoothing out the cast-in trademark for a super smooth look.

The front bearing housing is being smoothed. The bearing was removed to keep out the grit from all this sanding and polishing.

Far Left - Sand at right angles to the direction used before, so grit lines will disappear. Note the removed metal being thrown downward.

Left - Using wheel edge for tight places. We used a copper tube spacer to move wheel to end of motor adapter for best clearance.

Right - The completed alternator housing after being sanded smooth on the expander wheel only detailing remains to be done.

Right - Detailing hard-to-reach spots with abrasive cartridge rolls. Here they're on our #9000 Foredom Hi-Speed hand grinder.

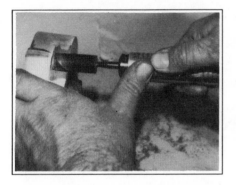

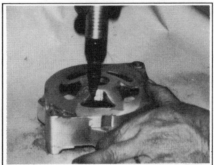

Far Left - Cartridge rolls come cylinder shaped and also tapered. Here the cylinder shape neatly smooths a mounting bolt recess.

Left - Tapered cartridge rolls make quick work of smoothing the casting marks from the front housing cooling air openings.

Right - After the sanding (polishing) is done, it's time to buff. A hi-speed (3600) rpm) motor is used. Apply compound lightly to wheel.

Far Right - The rear housing was buffed first. Again hold the part tightly. Apron protects since buffing is dusty and messy.

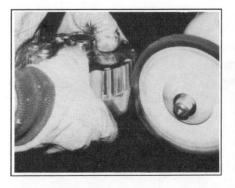

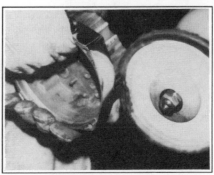

Far Left - In a few moments, see how the alternator housing begins to shine. Same principles apply to any aluminum part.

Left - More buffing produces a real shine. Check out the reflection of the buffing wheel against the housing. Note a good grip.

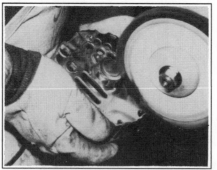

Left - Rear of housing is usually exposed so do a good job. Let the compound do the work, but don't overload the wheel..

Far Left - Working around the rear of the housing, note how the part is braced against the operator. Face shield is also worn. Always work safely.

Right - Final buffing is called "coloring" done with soft canton flannel wheel and White Rouge compound; gives brilliant finish.

Far Right - The finished product. Looks great and done at home. All that remains is to clean the parts and ready them for assembly.

Left - Assemble with relubed or new bearing and fresh brushes. Steel parts were spray painted. An easy afternoon's work. Join the fun!

Chrome Plating

Quite commonly, in the process of building of a custom car, it is necessary to have trim pieces, bumpers or other pieces of brightwork chrome plated before installation on the car. This is especially true if the pieces that were recovered from another car have been weathered or damaged, leaving them pitted or with original plating that has chipped and flaked off. But a trip to the plating shop is also necessary if you have made your own trim and need to have the shiny stuff put on it.

Nothing to worry about, right? Most major centers of civilization include at least one plating shop. But, just because there are shops available doesn't necessarily mean that all plating work can be counted on to be well done. There's good plating and bad plating, and you need to know how to ensure that the work you have done will be of high quality.

What we're going to discuss here are the things you need to watch out for when you visit your local plating shop, and questions to ask that disclose whether or not you can trust your valuable trim parts to a particular shop.

How To Find The Right Shop

Over the years, the plating industry has undergone a certain amount of progress. And, as with everything else, progress doesn't necessarily mean higher quality. In the case of plating, some aspects of progress have resulted in inferior quality. If, when you visit the plater, the shop is bustling with business and there are stacks of cartons containing faucets and other doo-dads that have nothing at all to do with automobiles, and an assembly line is robotically splashing parts from one tank to another with impersonal efficiency, look elsewhere. Assembly line work never results in the same kind of quality that comes from that personal attention of a craftsman giving individual care and attention to the parts being plated. So, from that standpoint, you are better off looking for a shop without all the bells and whistles of automated overhead hoists and computerized operation.

At the same time, you don't want the shop to be primitive in operation. There must be a certain amount of technology present in order to take advantage of the kind of progress that does enhance quality. For example, you want a shop that has the capability to do copper plating. In the old days, a quality chrome plating job consisted of a triple plating process that involved layers of copper, nickel and chrome. We'll discuss the fine points of chrome plating process in a moment, but in the meantime, realize that technology has advanced to the point that the copper plating isn't absolutely necessary in all cases. However, there are still many instances in which the copper layer must be included. This is especially true with zinc castings. Ask if the shop can plate zinc castings such as door handles, hood ornaments, etc. Zinc cannot take a plating of nickel directly on the bare metal without a coating of copper, so if they say they can't do zinc, look elsewhere.

When you walk into the shop, the man you talk with should have a good working knowledge of the kind of parts you are going to have plated. If a blank gaze crosses his face as you're explaining the brackets, door handles, hood ornaments and such that you want plated, look elsewhere. He must understand automotive parts, not just plumbing fixtures because there's a vast difference in how these pieces are treated.

Check the general appearance of the shop. If the place looks like something out of an Edgar Allen Poe story, look elsewhere. You don't want your parts subjected to the sloppiness and disorganization of a shop that resembles a dungeon. A well operated business will be reflected in the appearance of the shop, which will be clean and organized. Someone who doesn't take very good care of his business or his shop may not take very good care of your parts.

Regarding organization, ask the shop owner to explain to you what happens to your parts after you turn and walk out the door. If he can't explain a well organized procedure which instills confidence that you may one day see your parts again, look elsewhere. A good shop will have a set procedure, which may even include shooting Polaroid photographs of all the parts for later identification, tagging the pieces and placing them in bins or on shelves all together so they won't get lost.

Check the local reputation of the shop. Ask for references to people who have had work similar to yours done there in the recent past. Ask to see testimonial letters from satisfied customers.

Perhaps most important, ask to see some parts. Not the easy parts, but some difficult parts that will demonstrate how much care and attention to detail are given. Check to see that the plating is smooth and even, with no thin spots where the golden hue of underlying nickel shows through. Quality work will look new, with no pits or scratches showing even on old parts that may have been damaged or corroded in the past.

The Chrome Plating Process

When steel is being prepared for chrome plating, abrasives and buffing can be used on it to remove scratches and pits, leaving the raw steel with a mirror finish. After that, the piece can be plated with nickel and then with chrome. The chrome is a thin layer that alters the color of the nickel and adds corrosion-resistant coating.

If the piece to be the plated is either a zinc casting or is steel that has pits or other cosmetic problems, a layer of copper must be included in the process as the initial coat. This is necessary for zinc parts because nickel can't be applied to zinc directly. In the case of pitted or scratched parts, the copper can be applied in a thick layer to cover those cosmetic problems. Then the copper can be buffed, which flows the soft copper coating over the surface to fill in remaining flaws. Copper plating can be done repeatedly to obtain a sufficiently thick coating.

After the copper layer is perfected, the next plating process coats the part with nickel, and the final layer is chrome. This process is known as triple-chrome plating.

Doing Some Of Your Own Work

Can you do some of the preparation work to help cut costs in plating? That's a loaded question, because the next question is what kind of work can you do?

You'll note that earlier on we said that the piece to be plated had to be ground until it is mirror smooth. Plating does not cover scratches any more than paint covers scratches.

If you are merely having some plated items stripped and re-plated, don't bother to try and do your own polishing. If you are going to modify a piece of plated trim, you can have the chrome removed from the trim by the chrome shop, do the modifications, do the polishing, and then get the item replated. For example, suppose you want to cut and trim a bumper. You can go ahead and have the bumper de-plated, or you can just work on it. Saw or torch to the new shape you want, then grind the metal to shape. Next, use successively finer grades of sanding disc until you are leaving scratches so small you can't see/feel them. This will reduce the amount of time the plater has to spend polishing the piece. You will seldom be able to polish the item to exactly the standard needed, so just get as close as you can. Much of the cost of plating is in labor.

Don't leave big gaps and valleys and gouges and scratches and expect the plater to do miracles. If you want to do much of your own preparation, convince the plater you are serious, and then write to Jon Wright, Custom Chrome, Box 125, Grafton, Ohio 44044 or to Eastwood Company. They have special polishing equipment that you will find invaluable over a long span of years, in getting stuff ready for plating, in polishing stainless, in putting a hum on older chrome, in polishing aluminum, etc.

Quality Of Chrome

We're talking about the quality of the chrome as delivered to the plating shop, not the quality of the plating job as delivered to you. There has been some question lately about the quality of the chrome from foreign sources, whether African chrome is better than Brazilian chrome, etc. Jon Wright has been doing specialty plating for many, many years now, and he says that he can't see that there is a difference.

One source seems to be as good as the next. What might be happening is that a local plater who has problems doing a certain part may place the blame on the chrome, or the shop may be cutting corners on materials and/or labor and using the raw material as an excuse.

Care Of Chrome

Take care of the chrome plating you have and it will be around for a long, long time. Remember that the chrome is merely a surface coating, the nickel underneath is the shiney part. Keep the plating well waxed, and do not overlook putting wax or a clear paint over the part backside. Example: The bumper. The backside will have the same plating as the shiney front side, but it will be rough and look more like silver paint. Here the metal simply has not been polished and prepared. Coat this surface, and keep it coated, especially on the edges, and you can hold off deterioration.

If you get a scratch on the chromed surface, fill the gouge with with a clear paint, such as fingernail polish. Do this immediately so that corrosion does not get started. On rare occasion, the chrome overlay will peel away from the nickel, in this case it is vital to get the surface covered with clear paint, and keep it covered. This is nothing more than a very temporary fix, but at least it will preserve the surface from rust until the part can be replated.

Do not use a harsh abrasive to clean or polish chrome, the plated surface is not armor steel. Keep harsh chemical away front the plating, as well, and keep the plating well waxed. Do this and custom chrome plating will last a very long time, indeed.

Option

One option to chrome plating is to "black-out" all the normally plated parts. That is, to remove the plating and paint the pieces. The problem with this option is that the painted area (s) often get too "heavy", that is, the painted surfaces seem to form one huge mass of color. While this hi-tech approach may seem to be all the rage, it works best when done in moderation.

But the option to this option is to actually black-out the parts, but not with paint the same color as the body. For instance, for years the high dollar German cars have been painting the areas around the glass in honest soft black. The same thing might be done to a custom with outstanding results. Contrasting colors can be used, but here is is vital to choose the colors wisely, or the end result can look more like a circus wagon than a custom.

Another option is to use cadmium plating. Race cars have used cad plating for years, simply because a part that has been dipped in cadmium can still be Magnafluxed, while a chromed part cannot. And most racing organizations require certain certain highly stressed parts be Magnafluxed often during a racing season. Therefore, it might be desirable to cad plate various parts of the car, especially undercarriage and engine components. But be aware that cad plating will ultimately wear away. Also be aware that cad plating is available in a wide range of colors.

The question is often asked about doing chrome plating at home. Don't even bother. The chemicals involved in plating are listed as hazardous (and they most definitely are), so communities have strict laws about where a plater can, and cannot , be.

One type of finish that is sometimes used very effectively is hardly known at all . . . gunsmith bluing. This is usually available in every community, and it can have an amazing appearance.

With a minimum of tools and a little bit of practice, the backyard mechanic can easily learn to use plastic body filler to produce a finished body contour.

Plastic Body Filler

One of the important crafts for a customizer to learn is to work skillfully with body filler. Applying body filler is the quickest and easiest way to cover a dent, blend in body panels after welding or joining a fiberglass panel to the sheetmetal, or even to build up a major contour on the body.

The first step in the application of body filler is to clean and sand to bare metal the area to be worked on. Of course, if you're working on fiberglass, you won't be sanding to bare metal but to clean, raw fiberglass.

The next step is to mix just enough filler to take care of the chosen work area. Although we have witnessed the application of an entire gallon of body filler at one time (a feat not to be attempted unless you can afford to waste a gallon of filler and spend the rest of your life sanding), it is generally recommended to work with smaller amounts. This is especially true when you are learning. Don't try to do the entire body at one time, but choose a small area and work on that before moving to another spot.

In order to become hard, body filler must be mixed with a small amount of hardening cream. Follow the recommended ratio as printed on the container. When in doubt, a rule-of-thumb-ratio is to place a golfball size blob of filler on the palate and then blend in a 3-inch strip of hardener as it is squeezed from the tube. More hardener will cause the filler to cure faster, less will slow the process. A warm day will also speed the hardening.

Using a plastic body filler spreader, blend the hardening cream into the filler until there are no streaks of color. Everything should be uniformly colored. Work quickly, but be careful not to whip air into the mixture.

If there are grind marks on the metal surface being worked on, apply a thin layer of filler to fill these marks. Then follow immediately with the amount of filler necessary to fill the area until it is slightly above the surrounding metal. Smooth the filler, feathering the edges.

Allow the filler to cure. Curing time depends upon the mixture ratio and the temperature of the work environment. If you are working beneath bright, hot lamps, the filler may cure before you're ready.

Before the filler reaches complete hardness, it passes through a stage where it is about the consistency of cheese. This is when you can use a cheese grater file to remove excess filler quickly and easily. At this point, you must work swiftly because a in few more minutes the filler will be so hard that the cheese grater won't work. After that point, its sanding time.

When using the cheese grater and sandpaper, try to shape the filler to match the intended contour. Don't worry if you have to make a second or third application in order to bring the work area up to the desired contour. If it is necessary to apply additional layers of filler, wait until the previous layer has cured completely. Clean away any dust from sanding or filing the previous layer before applying the next one. Continue following the step-by-step procedure until:

1. The body filler runs out.
2. Somebody walks in and says, "It's Miller time."
3. You finish the job.

This is an art form in which the artist puts on 5 pounds of filler and then removes 4 pounds. At the end of the day, you think you are sweeping most of your effort into a dustpan, but the car looks beautiful.

Once the body filler has been finish sanded so that you can rub your hands over the side of the car with your eyes closed and feel no variation in contour, it's time to prime and paint.

Above - Before applying body filler to an area that has been welded, use a blunt drill bit to dig out all the slag or other rough particles from the weld.

Right - Mix plastic body filler a little bit at a time on an appropriate palate. Follow directions on the package to blend in the proper proportions of filler and hardener. Blend thoroughly until the colored hardener no longer leaves streaks in the filler, but everything is one color.

MIXING PLASTIC FILLER

When mixing plastic filler, remember that curing (hardening) time of the mixture will be dependent upon ambient temperature and the amount of hardener (catalyst) used. The mixing instructions for all brands of fillers are very similar, it is better to control the setting time with temperature than to change the ratio of filler to hardener. A couple of heat lamps directed to the work area are excellent sources of heat control in cool weather, in warm weather keep the work in a shady area.

If you're not sure about the set-up time, mix a small amount of filler and spread it on a disposable surface. You can tell by touch how fast the filler is curing. As it starts to set, the surface will feel resilient and tacky. This is the stage where you use the cheese grater for preliminary shaping. You'll have to work quickly, and you will note that the filler in this "soft" stage is easy to shape. Later, as it gets much harder, you must resort to sanding discs and shaping is much more difficult. So, take advantage of this malleable stage.

Obviously, since this cheese-grate period is not long, the smaller the area you are working, the better. It is not cool to lay on a large area of plastic and let it stay for several weeks before starting to shape. You'll really have to lay in the grinder effort.

When mixing filler, make sure it is a thorough mixing. The hardener will be a different color from the filler, and during mixing the compound will have a streaky look. Keep working the mix until it is a totally uniform color. If you apply plastic that is not mixed completely, you are in for problems that range from air bubbles to non-adhesion. Since the filler starts to cure from the very moment the hardener is included, you don't want to dally while mixing.

Do the mixing on a piece of glass, a regular plastic mixing palate, or some other inert surface. Do not use a convenient piece of cardboard. The cardboard will probably include waxes, and these can/do seep into the mix. The supply store will have a regular mixing board; our advice is to get one.

When digging filler from the can, use a stick only for that purpose. Do not contaminate this stick with mixed plastic, or you run the chance of having the entire can contents "kick" over a period of time.

After applying the filler, clean the mixing board and tools as the mixture is in the cheese grater stage. Wait too long and the mixture bonds to the mixing surface, making clean-up very difficult.

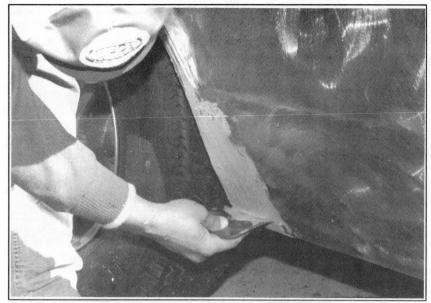

Left - Working quickly, but carefully, apply the body filler with a plastic spreader, following the contours of the car's body and feathering toward the edges.

Left Center - When the body filler has cured enough to become about the consistency of cheese, use a cheese grater file to remove excess filler.

Below - After the filler has "kicked" to the point that it is not longer workable with the cheese grater file, it's time to start with the long sanding board to achieve the finished surface.

Bottom Left - Prior to applying plastic body filler to a metal body, the surface must be ground all the way down to bare metal using a grinding disc that is rough enough to easily remove the old paint.

Bottom Right - Rather than simply filling rusted out body panels with a bunch of filler, the surface should be rebuilt with new sheetmetal first. The initial step is to grind away the paint and prepare the old surface to have new metal welded on.

PLASTIC FILLER QUALITY

Early on, plastic filler got a bad rap because there were so many different qualities available. There is still some of the less desirable filler available, almost always in the discount stores. Go for quality first.

Check with your local body repair shops as to good products in your area, and your supply stores will tell you which is the best to use. There is very difinitely a difference in how the plastic will work, how it will last, how it finishes, etc. Avoid problems: Get the best!

TOOLS

Application of the plastic will be with some plastic paddles, use different sizes for different areas to be covered. Cheese grater files come with flat and curved faces, you need one of each. For finishing the surface, use a very long sanding board. You can get double-action air sanders that will dramatically speed up the finish process, you can rent or borrow them if you don't want to buy. These are the straight-line sanders, not the rotary types. Plan on having to refill and sand again several times to get a perfect surface.

PLASTIC OVER PAINT?

Some of the new two-part paint systems include a primer that actually etches into, and bites, the bare metal. This is a very thin primer, not a filler surfacer, and it is part of a complete system. Bodymen have found that since this primer etches into the metal so well, it is possible to prime bare metal, then apply the plastic filler, and get a better bond on the filler than if it were applied directly to the bare metal

These etching primers are expensive, and they are usually very toxic (requiring the use of breathing masks/filters as even the most minimum precaution). Consult your local paint shop or paint supply store for information.

HOW MUCH IS ENOUGH?

The temptation with plastic filler is to use too much. Don't. The reason you see filler fall off a surface over time is almost always a case of too much filler. Work the metal surface until it needs only a thin coat of filler, then apply the filler in successive thin coats of build-up.

There are times when show-only car builders will literally apply plastic filler by the gallons. This may be ok for a car that is only on the show circuit, it doesn't work for something that is street driven and sees lots of temperature extremes.

Filler that is heavy at an edge, such as the door/hood/deck lid, will almost surely break away if it is thick.

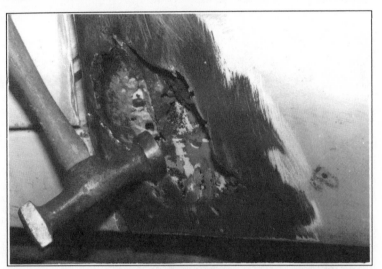

Top - After the new sheetmetal patch has been welded in place, use the grinder to smooth down any excess weld and clean the area to receive filler.

Center - Using a hammer, bend in the thin sheetmetal around the perimeter of the rusted hole. This hole can then be covered with new sheetmetal or a fiberglass patch. Plastic body filler is then used to finish the surface.

Bottom - When added strength is needed, such as when filling holes, a fiber reinforced filler can be used. Mix up just like regular body filler, then fill the area to be worked on.

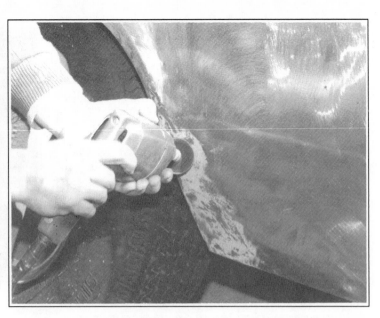

After spreading, the fiber reinforced filler is allowed to cure until hard. A cheese grater can't be used on this filler because of the fibers. When hard, use a grinder to shape the filler to conform with body contours.

Lead Fillers

Although leading is a dying art, it can be learned by anyone who is serious about the traditional methods used in body work. The tools and materials employed include a body grinder, pliers, gas welding set, body file, lead paddle set, tinning compound, lead, steel wool, disposable metal-shank brushes and safety glasses.

There seem to be two areas of total mystery in the custom car, areas that really become subjects of mastery with patience, experience, and some foreknowledge.

Lead filler, from whence sprang the custom nickname of LeadSled, was really about all we had for a body panel filler in the heyday of customs. That would be the period of about 1946-64. There were a few plastic and alloy fillers introduced right after World War II, but they were a far cry from the outstanding plastics of today. Those early "synthetic" fillers were so bad that many bodymen of the era simply wouldn't consider them as an alternative. Today, most of those bodymen are gone, and precious few people know the art of leading.

We won't go deeply into the subject here, that's something that will probably take up a series in our companion CUSTOM CAR Magazine. Because most all of the modern builders have very little need for lead...IF! If they use a MIG welder, if they learn how to shape replacement panels, and if they use plastic fillers sparingly.

Older cars included a lot of lead in the body, as produced by the factory. This would be in body seams, where panels were mated, and in areas where original stamping procedures simply couldn't create a needed shape. Most of the "factory" lead was installed with special leading guns, and it did/would sometimes crack after a number of years.

Lead is sometimes difficult to get today. Body lead, that is. Here, we are interested in a lead that is a 70/30 mix of lead and tin. We are NOT interested in the lead that radiator shops use! When you find body lead, expect to pay dearly for it, mostly only because it is a scarce item. You can locate it through some of the larger body shop supply stores, and some specialty mail order houses such as Eastwood Company list it in their catalogs. In fact, Eastwood also lists other lead working tools.

The lead will probably be available in a round or square stick, each stick will come in at close to a half-pound. The star-shaped cross-section stick is the best of all, if you can locate it. The shape presents a much larger surface to the heating torch, making the initial melting operation easier for the novice. For awhile in the early 1980, this style lead was available from a specialty supplier in the Minneapolis area, and advertised in restoration publications. It may still be available.

The tools you need for leading are: A body grinder to clean and rough the metal surface, pliers to hold steel wool, a gas welding set, a body file for lead, a lead paddle set (flat and round paddles) with beeswax, and if you're going to get serious, perhaps a special leading tip. This last piece of equipment slips over the gas welding tip and utilizes ambient air oxygen, saving on bottled gas. It also softens the flame.

Supplies you'll need: Lead, tinning compound (either liquid or granular), steel wool and/or disposable metal shank brushes.

Clean the metal surface with a body grinder or flexible sanding wheel. It is critical that the metal be absolutely clean prior to applying the tinning compound.

As with plastic filler, you don't want to gob huge globs of lead onto a panel. Use just as little amount of lead as possible. This is why you hear the really outstanding customizers brag about their hammerwelding techniques. What they are really saying is that they can finish the metal so good they need virtually no filler. Since lead is so expensive, you certainly don't want a lot of excess laying on the floor after filing.

A good rule of thumb when building the modern custom is to use lead wherever strength is needed, and a thin coating of plastic to get flawlessly smooth panels. And example of this would be to use lead over a welded seam that is likely to have a lot of working stress, or to use lead at the edge of a panel where the plastic could easily chip away.

Since an extremely few contemporary bodymen know how to use lead, you're probably not going to find someone who can give you a hands-on instruction. But this really is something that is fun to learn, and you can teach yourself. It is primarily a matter of experience, and the foreknowledge that heat warps metal. Simple as that.

Metal that is to be leaded must be absolutely clean. Even the little pits of a weld must be cleaned bright and shiney Because the clean metal must be completely and thoroughly covered with a lead tinning compound. This allows the lead to adhere to the metal. This tinning compound may be a liquid or a granular paste. With either, you must play the torch across the metal and heat it slightly. More on this later. The liquid is applied with the little throwaway metal handled brushes you get at most hardware stores for a dime each. The paste is applied with steel wool, which is held by pliers (because it gets hot rapidly).

Light the gas torch in the normal way, but use a medium to large tip. Just barely turn on the oxygen until you get a pair of blue flame cones (the yellow flame disappears). These long blue flames give a very low heat, which you need. If you use one of the special leading tips, you'll automatically get this blue flame when you light up. You are going to be using both hands, so be ready.

The area to be leaded has been thoroughly cleaned. Lightly "wipe" the soft flame over the metal, staying well off the surface with just the flame tip brushing back and forth. As you patiently heat the metal, dab the area with the tinning compound (brush or steel wool). As soon as the metal comes up to working heat, the tinning compound will flow onto the metal surface. The tinned area will have a bright silver color. Any metal that does not have this color will not be tinned, and lead won't stick there, so the key is to get everything tinned!!! Extremely important. Tin the area slightly beyond the edge of where you will apply lead.

Hopefully you've put all the stuff you will use within easy reach. Keep fanning the flame over the metal, and bring the lead bar into play. It seems to work best to hold the lead bar at a slight angle to the metal, and the torch flame at a converging angle. This way you fan the flame up the lead bar tip, then back across the metal, then onto the lead bar. Just at the point where the lead is going to melt (and drop on the floor!), the bar tip will change appearance slightly. Dab the lead onto the metal surface. A chunk of molten lead will adhere to the metal. You keep doing this until you have applied as much lead from the stick as you will need. Note: Always try to apply just a shade more lead than you will need. If you have to go back and add more lead, it can be frustrating trying to bring the earlier lead patch up to the correct heat (without having it melt too much and fall on the floor!!)

Here's a good piece of advice. Start your leading experiments by working on a flat surface, and only after you have control of the melting point do you go to a vertical surface.

Once you have your working lead "pile" on the surface, you keep the heat playing over the metal and you slowly soften the pile until it can be spread out with the lead paddle. Lightly heat the face of the lead paddle and rub the paddle across a beeswax surface. This will keep the lead from sticking to the paddle.

You're doing all these things at once, remember, with both hands, and you are continuing to keep the metal panel warmed.

Wipe the torch flame across the lead pile and touch the pile with the paddle. Just as soon as a tip of the pile starts to get to the "working" stage, ease up a bit with the heat. Use the paddle to spread the lead across the area. Because the lead pile will tend to hold the heat, once you get it to working temperature it will tend to stay malleable with less heat applied. But keep wiping the torch over the area, and keep spreading the lead, trying to smooth it to the correct contour with just the paddle. This will

reduce a lot of filing/grinding later, and saves a lot of lead. If you have an excess amount of lead, you'll run this up into a pile somewhere, and scrape it off with the paddle. If you have something clean on the floor to catch this excess, it can be used again (don't let it get dirty).

That's all there is to it!!! Let the lead cool completely, then work the surface with a file. These are special files, and once you learn how to use one, you will do lots of other work with them. They are vixen files that you also use on metal finishing if you are a real pro. Of course, the file won't cut as fast as a grinder, and that's the idea for the beginner. Later, you'll get good enough that you can do much of the finishing with a grinding disc.

The wax left on the leaded surface should be cleaned off with thinner. Chances are very good that you'll need to use a coat of plastic filler to get the perfect finish so common on today's cars.

Using lead is probably very archaic, but it is still a craft that anyone can do.

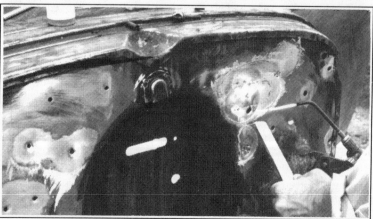

Top Left - Using a grinding wheel, clean the surface down to bare metal to eliminate everything that would interfere with the application of the tinning compound.

Above - Sweeping the torch flame gently across the metal to warm it slightly, apply the tinning compound with a metal-handled brush. Extend the compound slightly beyond the area to receive lead. If the area isn't tinned, the lead won't stick.

Left - Holding the lead bar at a slight angle to the metal, wipe the tip of the flame across the metal and up the tip of the lead bar to bring everything up to working temperature.

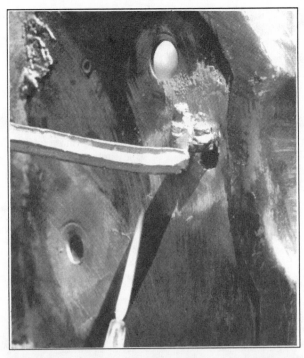

Top Left - Dab the warmed lead stick onto the warmed surface of the metal to deposit chunks of lead where needed. Always apply slightly more lead than you need because it's easier to remove than to add more lead later.

Above - Lightly heat the face of the lead paddle and then rub it on beeswax to prepare the paddle so the lead won't stick to it.

Above Left - Warm the lead until it reaches the working stage, then back off on the heat to keep the lead from falling off on the ground. Use the paddle to spread the lead across the working area.

Above Right - When working on a vertical surface, the first step is to simply mash the lead into the metal to get it to stick where it belongs.

Below Left - Next, keep working the lead and smoothing it out to a feathered edge that more than covers the working area.

Below Right - Use the lead file to remove excess lead from the working surface.

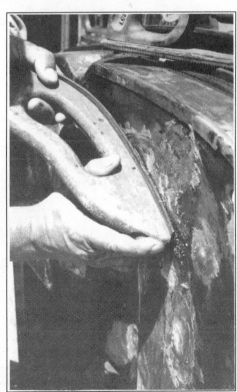

After gaining some experience, you can start to use a grinder in conjunction with the lead file for finish work.

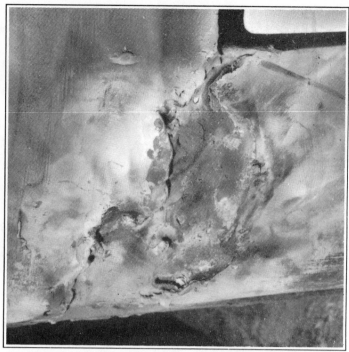

In older cars, it was common to have leaded seams, such as this one at the rocker panel. If damage has occured in that area, you need to melt the old lead out, reweld the seam and then relead.

Older cars often had leaded seams at the corners of the top. Inspect closely for cracks in these areas and relead if necessary.

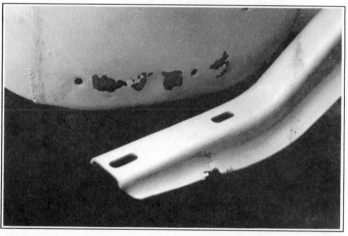

Above A double wall panel that has rusted through should be cut out and a patch of new sheetmetal welded in. Then lead the seams.

Left - When using a grinder to finish lead, use only a very fine grit sanding wheel. Take care to apply only the lightest touch because too much pressure can quickly eat away all the lead. If in doubt, finish sanding by hand.

UNIQUE; Different. Without equal. Words that describe the above customs. Even though the owners started with similar cars, the finished customs are totally different. Each car reflects the creativity and individualism of it's owner. Yet, all of the above cars do have one thing in common. Their owners all went to Night Prowlers, Inc. for their authentic fifties accessories. Why? Because Night Prowlers offers the largest selection, the lowest prices and the best service. Send two bucks for a catalog or call 417-682-3685 or 417-535-4885.

Night Prowlers

KUSTOM KEMP ACCESSORIES

P.O. BOX 551 · LAMAR, MO 64759

Molding Fenders

by Gene Winfield

Molding fenders to car bodies has been a part of rodding and customizing from the infancy of the hobby, and it is possible the procedure even influenced the Detroit car makers.

Most of the pre-1949 American cars utilized a clamshell fender arrangement, wherein the fenders (front and rear) bolted to the body. From 1949 on, it became fashionable to have the rear achieve the same smooth appearance with any of the bolt-on fenders, and it doesn't require a tremendous amount of body working experience. Patience, and a familiarity with welding, is the key. Follow along with the photos and I'll show you how we do this neat molding job in my southern California custom shop.

Above - Perhaps one of the most common of custom treatments for pre-1949 cars has always been the molding of the rear fenders to the body. The 1941-48 Fords are excellent foundations for this work, start by removing the fender welt and the chrome trim. The trim may or may not be retained. Tighten the fender bolts after the welting has been removed.

Below - Grind the paint away from the welting seam, and the trim line if necessary. Get the metal perfectly clean at this stage, and clean an area well to either side of the area to be welded and filled.

 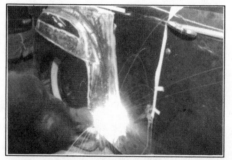 

Above Middle - Some customizers simply weld the fender to the body and then use lead or plastic filler to smooth the contour, we prefer to cut narrow strips of sheet metal to bridge the gap. This allows us to use only a thin coating of filler.

Above Right - Tack weld the filler pieces to the fender and the body. A MIG welder from Daytona MIG works well, sometimes we use the traditional gas torch. When using a torch, use care not to concentrate excessive heat and cause distortion.

Right - After the metal inserts are tack welded in place, shape the metal to a concave contour. Tap the shaping hammer with another hammer for a more precise control of the shaping.

Left - If the chrome trim is to be removed, fill the holes with weld. Some homebuilders try to cut corners by using plastic filler, we have found this not to be a satisfactory solution. If you are not a really good welder, you can use an asbestos base heat "dam" around the hold to reduce the distortion (mix asbestos and antifreeze or get the compound from Eastwood)

Below Left - Grind the welded area thoroughly. The cleaner the metal, the better the bond of either lead or plastic filler.

Below - A small rotary file will get into the small nooks and crannies of the weld seam. Take time to do this for best results. Always wear safety glasses while grinding.

Below - Only a thin coating of filler will be required. When using plastic, consult your local area bodymen for the brand best suited to your region. Follow mixing and application direction explicitly.

Below - Before the plastic filler "kicks" completely, it can be shaped with a cheese grater file.

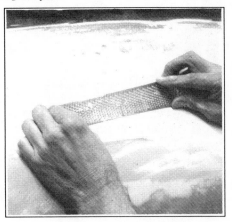

Below Left - After the filler has hardened completely, use a sanding board to get the final shape.

Below Middle - Any kind of duplicator can be used to check the continuity of the shape. Eastwood sells a good duplicator or you can make one by drilling a series of holes in a wood base and inserting metal/plastic rods.

Below - The finished molding job required only priming and paint, but the result is striking.

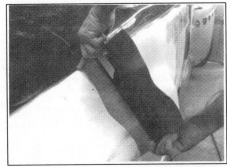

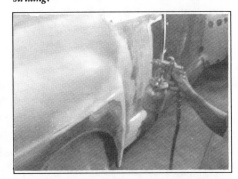

Fender Flares

When cutting flares from a modern car, get enough of the sheet metal beyond the flare area so that it can be worked into the flatter portion of the older car fender. Trim this metal and then use the flare as a pattern. Draw the mating edge onto the older fender making sure the flare is in the position you want. You're going to duplicate this procedure on the opposite fender, so work from some reference point.

Once the outline has been transferred to the older fender, cut away the original rolled bead opening, electric shears work best here.

Fender flares are extensions to the lip of the wheelhouse opening. Functionally, a fender flare permits a wider tire to be used without having the tread surface extend beyond the enclosure of the fender. This accomplishes two things: it keeps you from getting a traffic citation for the criminal act of exposing your tread; and it prevents dirt and rocks from being tossed up by the tread where it can do damage to the painted exterior surfaces of the car.

There are essentially two ways that fender flares can be installed on a custom car. One way is to design and fabricate a flare to match the combination of your imagination and the contour of the fender. This is an area where your creative juices can flow and you can design as mild or as wild a flare as you want.

The other method is to cut the flares off of an existing car (preferably one that has been relegated to the salvage yard) and attach them to your custom. This takes a bit of forethought and detective work to come up with flares that will complement your car's fenders rather than creating a visual argument between fenders and flares.

Whether you are designing your own custom flares or intend to use existing flares from another car, an artist's sensitivity comes in handy here. Overall proportion must not be violated.

Skinny fenders and fat flares (or vice versus) may look awful together. The general flow of sheetmetal must remain pleasing, as if the flares were a natural outgrowth of the fender itself. Subtlety is often a virtue when it comes to flares, and compatibility of shapes is also important. Rounded contours and sharp angles don't always look good together--too many different geometric shapes may conflict.

So, with all that in mind, let's leap into an examination of fender flare installation techniques by Gene Winfield.

Precise trimming so that the insert flare fits the old fender is done with a set of sharp hand snips.

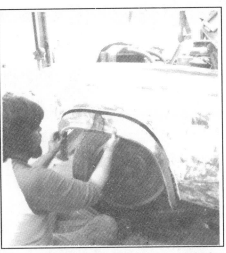

The new flare may need to be narrowed a bit for the older fender. Here we cut it at the halfway point and welded the ends back together before fitting the flare insert to the old fender.

The insert is tack welded in place. Lots of builders use the MIG "cold" welders (such as those from Daytona), but I still rely on my small gas welder. I spot weld the insert many places, then go back and add more spot welds, to reduce distortion.

I hammer weld the entire bead. This is not a difficult trick to learn, and it really separates the amateur bodyman from the professional.

The new fender flare insert is now in place, the bead hammer welded, and everything ready for the finishing work.

The entire area around the weld is ground smooth, well to each side of the weld seam.

Use a small rotary file or burr to get weld slag and grunge from the crevases. This is vital to get total filler adhesion.

The modern plastic fillers are exceptionally well suited to custom work, the idea is to use only a thin coat of filler.

The filler has been applied and sanded, additional filler added as necessary to get a perfectly smooth finish.

Rounding Corners

One of the more subtle customizing techniques that can help to expand on the theme of a curvaceous custom is rounding corners. When we talk of rounding corners, we are referring to the corners of a hood, doors or trunk lid. Some cars lend themselves better than others to having the corners of the doors, hood or trunk lid rounded. Cars that are especially suited to rounding corners are those with rounded fenders, hood and trunk lines. Also those cars with a sloping roofline that naturally produces side windows with a curved upper frame are ideally suited to having the corners of the doors rounded.

The work involved in rounding corners is not particularly difficult. It's sort of a cut-and-paste technique, cutting the squared corner off, moving it into the adjacent corner in the body and then welding it to the body. The tools necessary for a completed job are a die grinder with a cutting wheel, a mig welder, a grinder and the implements employed in applying and finishing body filler.

The technique is the same whether you're working on a door, a hood or a trunk. The critical thing is to create a curve that is smooth as it intersects the edges. As an example, we'll take a step-by-step look at how the corners of a door are rounded.

Beginning with a stock door, complete with square corner, describe a radius where the cut will be made. Try to make the radius look somewhat compatible with nearby curves such as those around the windows.

With a die grinder, equiped with a cutting wheel, cut along the scribed line. Be sure to wear protective goggles or a face shield during this operation. A hack saw works if you're patient.

Position the square corner of the cut off piece snuggly in its counterpart corner and tack weld it in place. Then follow up by completely mig welding the seams of the corner.

Even though the corner exterior sheetmetal is now in place, there is a gap behind the sheetmetal corner piece. This must be closed by welding in a strip of sheetmetal, blending it to form a smooth contour with the rest of the door jamb.

Weld the edge of the door where the corner was cut off to seal the inner and outer sheetmetal. Grind all the welds until they are even with the surrounding sheetmetal.

If the work has been done carefully, a minimum of body filler will be needed. Fill the imperfections with body filler, allow it to cure and then sand. Finish by priming and painting.

The hood corners are rounded exactly the same way, whether the corner is to be minimal or really radical. Since most corners will be minimal on a hood, the procedure is exactly the same as the door (so is the deck lid). The inner support structure for most doors/hoods/deck lids will already be slightly rounded, so that no work there is necessary. However, if a really radically rounding job is going to be done--a job that is most often associated with a pancake hood or a recontoured deck lid-- after the initial cut is made the remaining inner support structure must be

It is very popular to round the corners of custom car hoods, deck lids, and doors. The method of doing this is similar in all cases, cutting a piece from the hood/deck/door and moving it to the adjacent area. When chopping a top, as on the 1949-53 Mercury, it is sometimes desirable to slant the door posts and round the door corner at the same time.

"closed off" with a strip of sheetmetal welded between support and outer panel. Be sure to tack weld this piece in many places before final welding, and check alignment often. The piece of outer panel with inner structure attached is welded to the body or fenders and trimmed off the same way.

All of this may sound complicated, but it really is quite simple. While it can be done with a gas or arc welder, the MIG is far superior because of speed and minimal metal distortion.

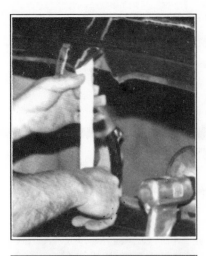

Left - In the method used by Dick Dean, a notch is cut on top for the angled door post to fit in, this notch can be cut smaller and trimmed to fit the post.

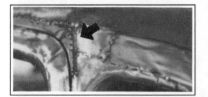

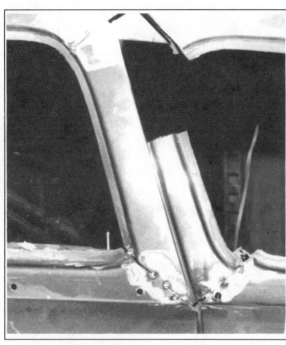

Left - The door window frame is positioned and tack welded in place, then the door post insert is tacked in place. When everything is aligned, the corner that is cut from the sharp window frame is welded to the body (arrow). With very careful welding and grinding, very little filler is needed, try to have no filler at all (except lead) on any edges where it can break off.

Below - The rounded corner is only a very subtle change, but it goes with the other round corners common to most cars, note here that the door corner complements the window curve. A small change, but it has a big part in overall design harmony.

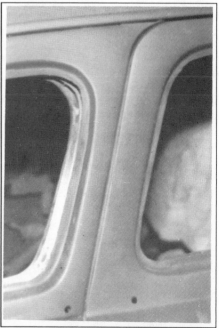

Skirts

Left - Flush fitting skirts are a great way to visually assist in lowering the body and covering all but a few inches of tire sidewall.

Below - Dick Dean has fiberglass skirts for Mercs, and demonstrates here how to install them flush.

Bottom - The key to keeping the skirts securely fastened to the fender is installation of a strong support bracket. This one is just a length of angle that is welded on the inner side of the fender, just above the opening.

Although it isn't a hewn in rock dictum, the skirt and the custom seem to go hand in hand. Early on, most customs had to make do with skirts pirated from other vehicles, or use aftermarket items. As a general rule, these skirts came as teardrops, blunt end teardrops, for boxes. Later came the very long Foxcraft styles, but all were add-on's. They fit over the fender panel, while some of the nicer semi-style skirts coming on new cars of the 50s and 60s were of the flush fit style.

Since the flush fitting skirt is all the rage, we'll confine our interest to them for this book. We called on Dick Dean to show how a set of skirts can be made to fit flush, and this same procedure would hold for nearly any size of skirt. The larger the skirt and resulting fender opening, the more the need for a really strong support structure built into the fender panel.

Although this seems to be a complicated piece of work, it really isn't difficult. The key is to have a basic knowledge of welding, and have access to a MIG welder. The skirts can be currently available aftermarket items, something from the wrecking yard, or you might even want to make up your own (See Custom Car magazine, volume 1, number 1).

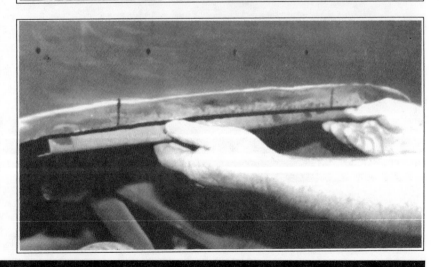

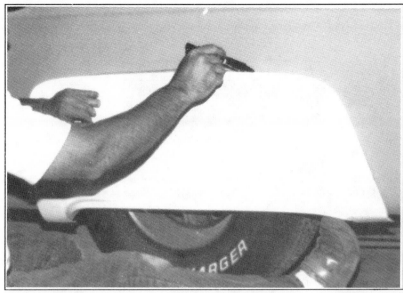

Left - To mark for cutting away the fender so a skirt can be flush-fit, hold the skirt up against the fender and draw the outline.

Below Left - Using a die grinder and cutting disc, follow the outline and cut away the fender lip that is unneeded.

Below - If you were involved in doing several flush skirt installations on Mercs, you might want to save the cutout portion of a fender to use as an outline template.

Bottom Left - Hold the skirt up to the cutout and mark the position of the studs that will protrude through the support bracket on the inside. Then transfer these marks to the bracket and drill. Bolts hold the lower lips of the skirt to the fender.

Bottom Right - The skirt in the foreground has been finished, with the mounting studs and support bar glassed in on the inner side, while the background skirt is yet unfinished.

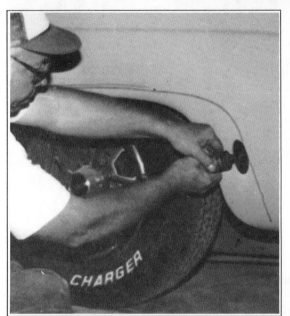

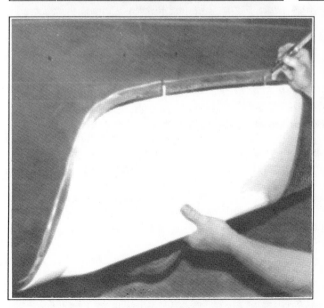

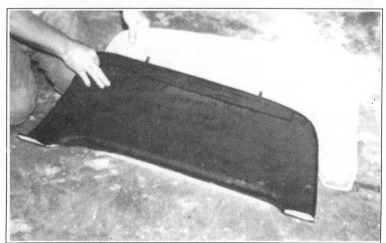

Hood Scoops

By Gene Winfield

The more traditional Mercury customizing tricks here, including filled splash pan, tunneled headlights, and rolled hood corners. The unusual starts to show with the imitation hood scoop on each hood side, a theme that can be repeated toward the rear of the car if desired.

Functional scoops have a heritage in racing. Their purpose is to direct the flow of air onto or around certain components that benefit from the greater flow of air. The purpose may be to feed more air to the engine intake system, or to pass air through the engine compartment for cooling. Likewise, scoops have been designed to flow air over the brakes to cool them and help prevent heat-induced fade.

. . ."The customizer has much greater freedom than factory designers, and there is hardly anything that attracts the admiring eye more than tastefully executed scoops."

Over the years, scoops have shown up on almost every part of factory-built automobiles. Sometimes they served a purpose, but more often the purpose was only to enhance appearance, to make the car appear to have more performance than reality (or Detroit) would permit.

Of course, the customizer has much greater freedom than factory designers, and there is hardly anything that attracts the admiring eye more than tastefully executed scoops. Today's customizer can choose to make scoops functional or to make them for purely cosmetic reasons. Often, the only difference is that the sheetmetal behind the scoop has been opened up to allow the air to flow through. Follow along with this sequence as Gene Winfield creates a set of hood scoops.

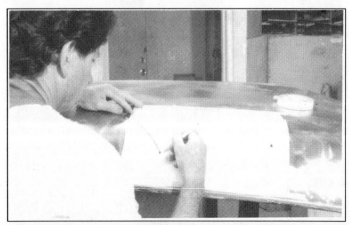

Step one is to design the scoop on cardboard. With the cardboard laid up against the contour of the hood, it is easier to see how the finished scoop will look.

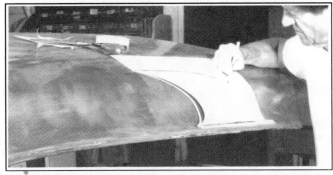

By flexing the cardboard and taping it to the hood, Gene creates the actual scoop opening effect on his template. With the opening completed, Gene works out the contour of the rest of the scoop.

Now the cardboard template is flattened out and the outline is transferred to a piece of sheetmetal. By reversing the template, both left and right scoops can be traced onto the sheetmetal.

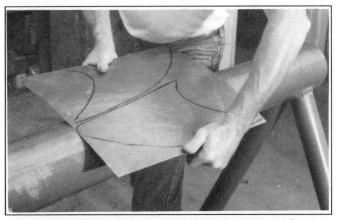

The sheetmetal is worked over a length of pipe to create the proper contour. By bending the sheetmetal before cutting out the two scoops, it is easier to ensure that both will have equal contours.

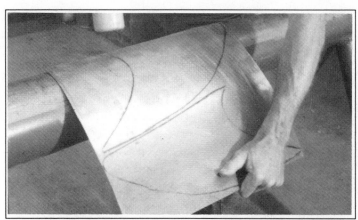

A soft mallet can be used to encourage the sheetmetal to conform to the desired shape. The important part here is to work the metal so that it has a uniform curve all the way across.

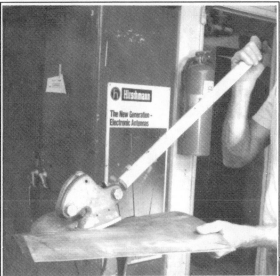

Right - Hand shears can be used to snip out the curved portion of the scoop opening. Be careful to avoid metal distortion around the radius of the scoop opening as you are cutting.

Above - The two scoops are separated so that each can be worked on individually. A large shear makes this work fast and easy.

Right - After the scoop has been completely cut out of the sheetmetal, the lip of the opening can be rolled inward to create a smooth scoop mouth.

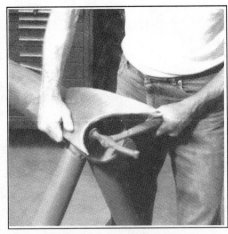
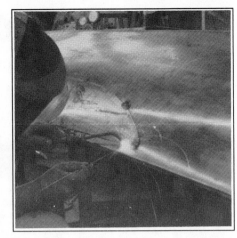

Above Left - Hammer and dolly come in handy to gently work any kinks out of the contour.
Above Center - Final touch-up of the rolled scoop opening can be accomplished with a hammer. Holding the scoop over the curve of the pipe helps maintain the contour of the sheetmetal while working on it with the hammer
Above Right - The finished scoop is now tack welded to the hood in the predetermined location. Spot welding or stitch welding helps avoid heat distortion to the hood or the scoop.

Carefully mig weld the entire perimeter of the scoop to the hood. Procede an inch at a time, then allow the metal to cool to help prevent distortion.

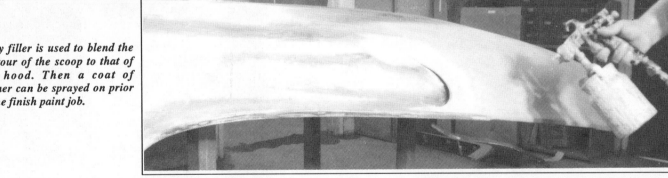

Body filler is used to blend the contour of the scoop to that of the hood. Then a coat of primer can be sprayed on prior to the finish paint job.

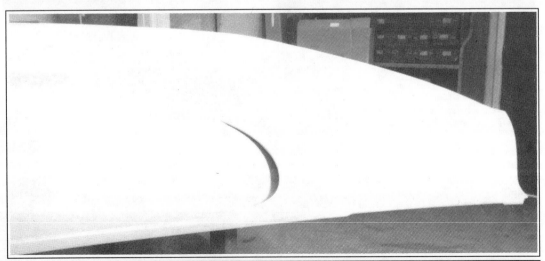

The end result of this exercise is a fine looking, although non-functional hood scoop. To make the scoop functional, an opening can be cut in the hood behind the scoop to permit air flow to the engine compartment.

Fender Scoops

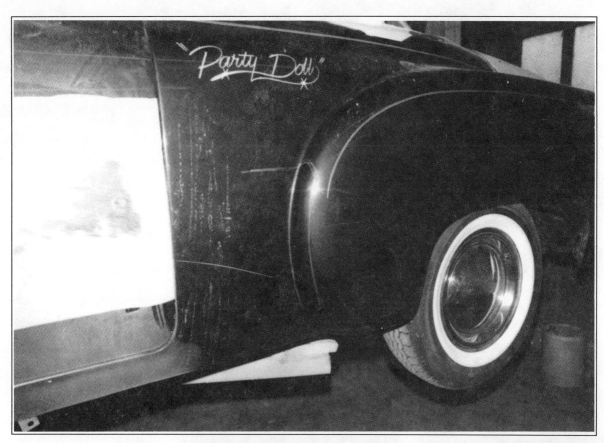

D uring this sequence of photos, Party Doll gets a new set of non-functional scoops in the leading edge of the rear fenders. If these scoops are left open at the rear, rather than being blocked off, air would be directed into the wheelwell where it could serve to cool the brakes.

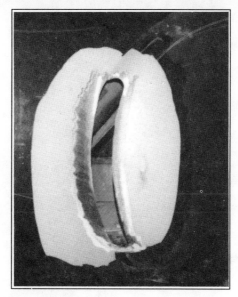

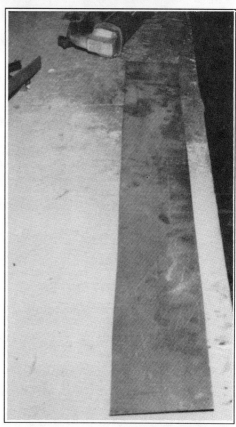

Above - The outline of the scoops has been drawn on the forward edge of the rear fenders in preparation for cutting the opening for the scoops.

Right - Paint and primer have been ground away to expose bare metal in the work area. The scoop opening has been cut out, allowing us to see the chassis behind the fender.

Far Right - A long strip of sheetmetal is the raw material from which the scoop box will be made.

A pair of Vice Grip clamps are used to hole a length of pipe that serves as a radius form for the upper and lower ends of the scoop box.

The sheetmetal strip is wrapped over the pipe to create the desired radius for the scoop box at upper and lower ends. The encouraging blows of a soft mallet help achieve this result.

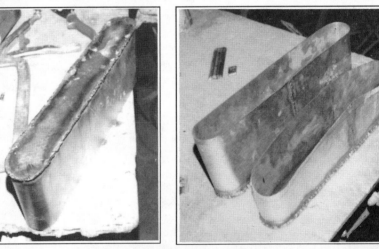

Above - With both ends of the scoop box formed, the sheetmetal strip is welded where its ends meet.

Center - Because this is to be a non-functional scoop, the back side of the box is closed off by welding a piece of sheetmetal across it.

Right - In order to make the box conform with the contour of the leading edge of the fender, it must be cut down to create a rounded forward edge. These two boxes can be compared for an idea of how they look before and after.

Below - The scoop box can now be tack welded in place. Note that the edges of the box don't conform exactly to the contour of the fender, so some grinding is necessary.

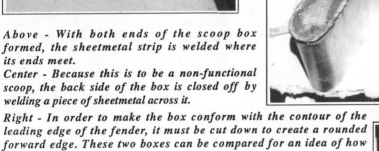

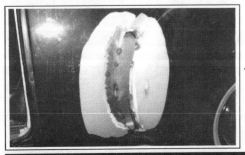

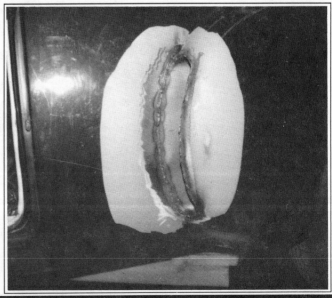

Right - Initial grinding complete, the box fits the fender pretty well. The entire perimeter of the box is welded, but carefully as to avoid distortion to the fender.

Now the final grinding has been done, resulting is a clean, sharp appearance for the scoop perimeter. Note that the contour of the body flows smoothly into the scoop box without interruption.

Above - Body filler is used as blending agent to make the scoop opening smooth and in perfect conformity with the fender and body contours. Primer is followed by the finish paint job.

Filling Holes

The bane of any customizing attempt seems to be the problem of filling holes. Holes where the side trim was attached, holes for the deck lid handle, holes for the door handles, holes for the hood ornament...the list seems endless. And, on an older car, when all the excess chrome trim is removed, it looks as though the car were hit with machine gun fire!

Interestingly, filling holes is more tedious and time consuming than it is difficult. It is something that the amateur can attempt with confidence. With the result that by the time half the car is done, the amateur will be an expert.

But, before starting on the hole filling job, do some careful eyeballing. Perhaps you will be replacing original side trim with different trim that happens to be in the same place. Lots of the original holes might be used. Saves a lot of work. Also, if you are going to do some major type of bodywork, such as a section job, chances are the section to be removed will be right through the trim area. In short, do some planning ahead.

There are several ways to fill sheetmetal or fiberglass body holes. With the glass body, you obviously use fiberglass as a filler. No big deal. But you can also use glass to fill sheetmetal body holes. But, with fiberglass you can have problems. First, the how-to. You need to get to the metal behind the holes. Clean this surface best way possible and add a fiberglass patch across the hole. You want this patch to last indefinitely. After the resin in this patch has cured, rough up the outside surface slightly and apply a quality body filler. For a larger hole, anything larger than a pencil size, use the Tiger Hair type reinforced filler, finishing with regular filler.

The problem with this type of hole filling is that too often the filler will "let go" and you end up with a circle crack. Some builders are extremely successful with fiberglass filler for holes, but the large majority prefer to weld the holes. We have seen experiments with dimpling the holes and adding large diameter rivets, then using plastic filler, but so far this hasn't proven really good.

With welding, super caution must be used to minimize panel distortion. The rule of thumb is to use the coolest welding technique possible, and even then be prepared to do a bit of panel working to get everything perfectly smooth.

Holes can be welded with a gas torch, a TIG/MIG arc, or even a regular arc machine. We have successfully welded holes shut with the StitchWelder sold by Eastwood, which is a form of rapidly pulsing arc welding. Here, let's concentrate on the two most common forms of welding gas and MIG.

The idea is to have the coldest weld possible. If you are stuck with only a gas torch, then remember that you want to use the smallest flame possible (meaning you use a small torch tip), so reduce the gas pressures at the regulator. And use a small rod diameter. Refer to the chart on the next page. In the interest of economy, you can use wire coat hangers or even ordinary hay bailing wire, since this is not a strength area.

Grind the paint from the hole edge back about an inch or so. If you can, build up a heat dam around the hole. We make our own by mixing crumbled asbestos with anti-freeze, to create a paste. An inch or slightly less from the hole diameter, make a dam about 1-inch thick and 1-inch high, the material slightly on the wet side. If you keep this mixture sealed, it will stay moist indefinitely. If you don't want to make up you own, get a similar heat control substance from the Eastwood Company.

You can weld the small trim holes directly. You might be tempted to use brass...don't, because it is very difficult to get a perfect paint bond over the brass. With the small gas flame and small rod, weld a bead around the hole perimeter, in a kind of spiral motion, one bead overlapping the other until the hole is plugged. It won't take long and you'll have a knack for this.

Warning: Be sure and remove all upholstery from the body, because the quick way to a fire is to weld up holes with the upholstery in place.

If you will gas weld a larger hole, such as the door handle hole, cut a piece of sheetmetal larger than the hole, but in a rectangle. This way, the piece of metal can be barely slipped through the hole but will lap at either side. Tack weld a piece of wire to the center of this patch and work the metal through the hole. The wire is used to pull the metal flush against the backside of the hole. Just barely melt an edge of the hole metal to the backup piece, then you can free a hand to use welding rod and tack weld around the hole diameter. Now, your option is fill the patch with weld, or use a filler (either lead or plastic). If you will use plastic, you'll get the best results if you weld the entire perimeter solid. Again, you can somewhat control distortion by using the heat dam mentioned above.

When grinding away excess weld, go easy with the grinder because you can create enough heat with one to cause panel distortion.

It is possible to actually solder holes shut, because this is just a variation of body leading. A benefit of using solder is that there is very little heat generated. It is cheap, and easy to do.

After grinding all paint well away from the hole, countersink the hole slightly with a larger diameter drill bit. You would also chamfer the hole if you were going to use body lead, as this gives a slightly larger face for the solder to bite into. Use acid-core solder and a soldering iron. Start around the hole edges, same as with gas welding, and gradually spiral inward until the hole is filled. This works ok on the very small trim holes, for the larger holes make up a backing plate from cleanly ground metal and have someone hold it against the panel while solder is applied to the outside. Finish off with a file or sander.

If you're going to do any amount of bodywork at all, go ahead and pop for one of the neat MIG home welders available from either Daytona MIG or HTP America. If you're just going to be doing light work, you can do an excellent job with the little 110 models. These are the ones that work off ordinary household electricity. If you are going to get a bit more serious, go ahead and get the 220 unit and wire your garage to suit. These welders are wire feed from an automatic spool, and they use an inert gas to shield and cool the weld area. You'll quickly learn how to weld with them, especially on sheetmetal.

With a MIG welder, you set the temp just high enough to make the wire stick, but cold enough to prevent metal burn-through or distortion. You can tack weld a metal patch to the larger holes, and you can sort of "gob" the smaller holes full of weld. Even though this is a so-called cold weld, alternate tack welds to really keep heat build-up minimized. When you are learning, you'll tend to get on more than enough weld material, so you end up grinding a lot off. With experience, or by the time you reach the other side of the car, you'll be laying on just enough weld. With the MIG welder, you won't have a "dirty" weld either, where you must use a lot of clean-up later before using a filler. Remember not to overheat the metal while grinding.

Filling holes is not difficult, just tedious.

CHART			
Metal Thickness	Rod Diameter	Oxygen PSI	Acetylene PSI
1/16"	1/16 - 3/32"	4	4
1/8"	3/32 - 1/8"	5	5
1/4"	5/32 - 3/16"	8	8
3/8"	3/16 - 1/4"	9	

**The Only Company Devoted Exclusively
To Manufacturing Power Window Kits For Older Vehicles**

**Specialty
Power
Windows**

(912) 994-9248 Technical Information
1-800-634-9801 Factory Sales Desk
1-800-728-3881 West Coast Sales (CA)
FAX (912) 994-3124

Route 2, Goodwyne Road, Forsyth, Georgia 31029

Sectioning

Photos by Gene Winfield

Sectioning is to the body as chopping is to the top. The result is a lower profile, achieved by slicing a horizontal section out of the entire body. It's like taking one layer out of a layer cake. As in all other aspects of customizing, sectioning must be approached with an artistic eye and sensitivity for proportion. Stock vehicles are generally built around a proportion of 2/3 body and 1/3 greenhouse. Either chopping or sectioning changes this proportion. If both chopping and sectioning are done the car can retain a somewhat stock proportion and yet be an unmistakable custom.

Although there are some cars that look dynamite after a moderate section but without also chopping the top, other cars seem to need both at the same time. However, in this case, the top chop should be considered only after the car has been sectioned. Work the body first, then make the greenhouse proportional to it.

One way to see in advance what the proposed sectioning job will look like when it is finished is to take a photograph of the vehicle from the side and then cut the picture lengthwise through the body. By overlapping the two pieces of the picture so that the body is shortened through the midsection, you can see a rough approximation of the result. Chop the top of the photograph in the same manner and you can get a pretty good idea of what the final custom will look like after the car has been chopped and sectioned.

The most common problem with sectioning is the temptation to remove too much. Generally speaking, a 3 to 5-inch section is plenty.

One of the first steps in sectioning is to decide exactly what layer of the cake to remove. If the car has distinctive and desirable body side sculpturing which you want to retain, the sectioning will have to take place either above or below this area. However, if the upper and lower portions of the body are fairly equally divided by this side sculpture, it may be necessary to remove a layer both above and below in order to maintain a

pleasing proportion. That is a complication that needs to be worked out in the mind of the owner before work begins.

For the sake of simplicity, however, let's assume that the body is to be sectioned along a single line. Ideally, the section can be removed along a line that will permit the upper body and lower body contours to mate closely when the two parts are rejoined. Now, follow along with these photos of a complete section job.

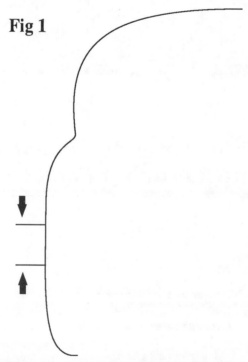

Fig 1

To begin, two horizontal lines that are the appropriate distance apart are marked around the entire car, indicating the section to be removed.

Page 86 *How To Build Custom Cars*

Top Left - Using thin masking tape, the body is marked to indicate where the surgery will be performed, careful measuring will ensure that the cutting is always parallel.

Above - The door has already been sectioned, and clearly shown how much lower the body profile will be in relation to a stock door cavity.

Left - First, the outer body panels are cut away. Then the upper part of the body is supported while the inner panels are cut away. The upper body can then be lowered into place.

Right - With the upper body lowered to mate with the lower body, it is evident that the proportion between body and greenhouse has been drastically altered. Sometimes this is as far as a customizer will need to go, but often a top chop is necessary to regain the original proportion. In this instance, the wheelhouse needed to be radiused quite a bit for tire clearance.

Left - This is a fine example of a sectioned '58 Chevy in which the stock greenhouse has been retained. The body was sectioned about 6 inches right through the beltline.

Right - Sectioning the firewall can be tricky. The section line must circumnavigate essential equipment that is attached to the firewall, zigging and zagging yet retaining the same amount of section removal as the body.

Below - If you look closely, you can see how the upper body is supported on jack stands and boards to maintain a consistent distance from the lower body while the inner panels are cut.

Bottom Left - After the upper and lower portions of the body are brought together, the seam is carefully mig welded to avoid metal distortion.

Bottom Right - Using snips, sheetmetal panels are cut to fill the gaps as the molded-in rear bumper is constructed.

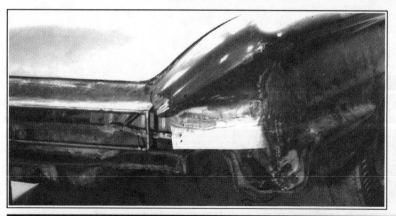

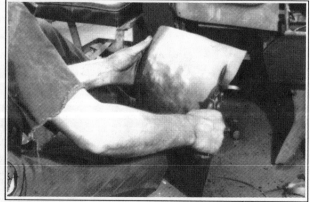

Constructing the custom molded-in rear bumper required fabrication and joining of several different pieces to come up with the desired contour. All the separate bumper pieces were welded together off the car, hammered into shape and then welded to the car. All the molding was done with sheetmetal in this case.

Left - Final blending in of the bumper to the body panels was executed and all the seams treated to a dose of grinder.

Below - It's hard to argue with results that look this good. In addition to all the various customizing techniques employed, sectioning left this '58 looking low-down and snakey.

Channeling

While chopping tops is common practice to both street rods and customs, the practice of channeling is more a part of hot rods than of customs. Conversely, sectioning is more a part of customs than rods. But, as with everything automotive, there are plenty of exceptions to the rule.

It is very plausible to channel a custom body over the frame; the question comes as to whether or not it is practical. The only reason we chop/section/channel cars is to get the body profile lower. While we are getting down out of the wind, we try to make all the proportions pleasing. Unlike chopping or sectioning a body, a channel job seems only to change relationship of the body to the ground. Thus, the amount of body channel is dictated more by ground clearance than anything. The top chop may work best at between 3-5 inches, and the section may be best at between 4-6 inches, the only real factor to determine channel is amount of ground clearance and human body room.

The person who is over 6 feet tall will probably be thinking of a channel maximum of about 4 inches, while someone who is shorter can go for 6 or so inches. In reality, the channel will probably be about the depth of the frame, or around 5 inches.

A good rule of thumb: Try the car on for size before making a final decision on channeling.

If the vehicle will have the "old" body set on a newer frame (a '49 Merc body on a '72 Chevelle frame, for example), the body can be channeled at the same time. Especially if the late model flooring is being used.

The body is severed from the flooring completely around the perimeter of the floor (where the floor meets the body sides). While this cutting can be done with a Sawzall or other kind of saw, careful use of the cutting torch works fine. At the firewall, make a vertical cut straight upward from the frame to a point just above the slanting footboards. Then, make a sectioning cut across the firewall the depth of the desired channel.

Drop the body over the frame and block it into place. Check all the spaces for the correct amount of channel, then begin to weld in the spaces with sheetmetal. If the channel is 5 inches, the sheetmetal inserts will be exactly 5 inches wide. Weld these inserts to both flooring and body (where the floor originally attached). Now the body is again one piece, sealed against dust and water.

A problem will arise at the rear fender wells, which will have been cut away from the floor. Now, the inner wells must be trimmed and welded back to the floor. However, and this is important, if the fender wells drop too low over the tires there won't be enough tire clearance. Solution is to raise the fender

Channeling lowers the body in relation to the floor, resulting in a step up from the door sill to the floor. Sheetmetal bridges the gap produced by lowering the body, and lots of square tubing should be welded between the lower portion of the body and the floor for added bracing.

wells in the body. At the front, the fender inner splash aprons must be trimmed for fit. Fender tire openings may be radiused higher in the fender for tire clearance, and the radiator may need to be repositioned or reworked for hood clearance. The steering mast jacket will need to be relocated downward. If the steering gearbox is swiveled to drop this mast, the pitman arm will not be in correct alignment. The best thing to do is replace the older steering system with a later model gearbox that will allow use of a universal joint in the steering shaft. This way, the gearbox mounts normally, yet the steering shaft can be repositioned lower. Generally speaking, any time a car is channeled, the seat risers must be removed. This places the seats right on the floor.

Lowered seats often lead to uncomfortable driving position unless the area below the knees is built up to give additional leg support. Sometimes, a channeled car also requires seats that lay back slightly. This is for headroom as well as back and leg support.

Do not do a channel job unless you fill in all the space between floor and body with new metal. Also add some more bracing between original floor level and the body. Many otherwise great customs have been ruined by a sloppy channel job. This is not work that requires a tremendous amount of experience, but it does require patience. Fortunately, since you're working mostly with heavier metal that is not cosmetic, you can channel a car with far less hassle than doing a section or chop job.

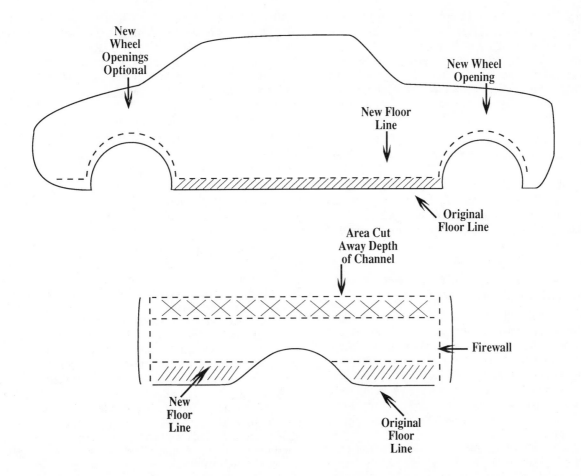

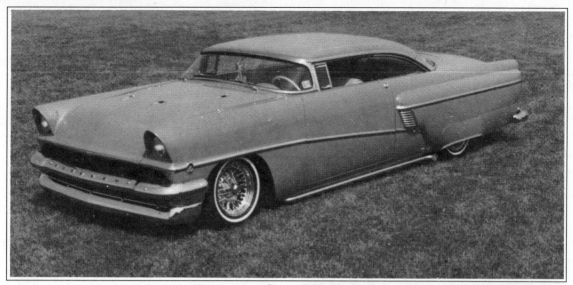

Photos by Gene Winfield, Dave Simard, Calvin Mauldin

The key to automotive design - indeed, to any kind of design - is proportion. Balance of all visual components. Artistic "feel". This is where the really good custom car is so set apart from the average or poor custom.

As we have mentioned elsewhere, a rule of thumb for body proportion is one-third "greenhouse" and two-thirds sheet metal. The vehicle top is about one-third as high as the body. But, as with all rules, this is a very flexible thing that simply cannot be cast in stone. This is why certain cars look outstanding with a certain kind of top chop, while others look better with a body section. And it is why nearly every vehicle looks better very close to the ground.

This chapter will not be, can not be an absolute manual for chopping a top. In fact, we have a complete 200-plus page book entirely on this vast subject (available Fall, 1989). In this chapter, we will take an overview of the subject and still be as specific as possible. While it is true that every vehicle has different problems with a top chop, it is also true that the solutions to these problems are very similar. This means that whatever applies to one chop, be it for a coupe, a sedan, a pickup, and so on, will apply to most chops.

The real keys to a successful top chop are planning, patience, and a willingness to do something over to get it correct.

So, start with planning If it holds true that most cars look best with a top area about one-third that of the body sheet metal, this is a good start. It seems that most top chops will be in the area of 3-4 inches. Some will be more, some less. Your job is to determine exactly how much is right for your car. If you have seen similar cars, then you have the advantage of working from those parameters. For now, let's assume that you only know that the majority of cars seem to look best with the chop average of 3-4 inches. You can get a very good idea of how much you should chop your car by using a photo or drawing that has been cut apart. Shoot a straight side view of the car, and a three-quarter front/rear, in black/white film. These can be Polaroid, for convenience. Determine the approximate scale of the photo,

and cut the equivalent of 3-4 inches from the top. You'll end up with some blank spots that need to be filled in with ink pen, but you can then decide if you want to have more or less of a chop. Modify the photos or drawings until you have the look you want.

While you're at it, this is a good time to learn what "pancaking" the top metal will do. On the older cars, say from about 1955 back, the sheet metal above the doors will usually be highly crowned. If you want to slim down the top' appearance, cut the photo/drawing apart to flatten this area. If you like the new flatter appearance, realize that you can cut the flatter sheet metal from a late model top and use it as an insert in the earlier tops. This tends to make a top look as though it is chopped much more than it actually is. You also lose headroom, so keep that in mind.

This working with a photo or drawing is only a rough approximation. Once you cut the top from the body, you can raise or lower it (the top section) to get an even better idea of just how much the final chop should be. Obviously, this is where a pair of extra hands are useful.

When chopping a top, it must be decided where the top supports will be changed or left alone. For the sake of clarity, call the windshield posts the A-posts, the door posts (those units behind the door) the B-posts, and the area where the top attaches to the quarter panels (between rear side window/rear door and back window) the C-posts. All this for reference only. On the very early car bodies, such as the Ford Model A, all of these areas are nearly vertical, so that when a section is removed from the posts, realignment is simple. When the windshield posts and rear of the top are slanted, however, the problems start. When a section is taken from the A-B-C post areas of the slanted top, the top can only realign at one of the three post areas but not any two or three. If you bring the top straight down and align the door posts, the windshield and back glass areas are way out of alignment. The windshield posts must be V-notched in this scheme, which often makes the top seem out of proportion. Obviously, if the back window area is aligned, the windshield posts are even more radically misaligned.

Top chops have stock windshield slant and laid down rear windows, or "Bonneville" highly slanted windshields. Dick Dean starts the process of chopping a Mercury, this particular body style needs rear window slant just right or the job looks out of proportion.

For the most part, customizers choose to align the windshield posts, which means the B- and C-post areas must then be reworked. NOTE: It is possible to make a hardtop from a two-door by removing the B-post area. This is considerable extra work, but it is done and the results can be very good. A lot of work is required to make operable side windows.

Remember that any section removed from the top posts is a horizontal removal. But, when making the marks for the cut, the marks must be parallel to each other for realignment.

Before starting a top chop, remove all upholstery in the area, including the entire headliner. Also remove all glass and inner garnish moldings. If the top is flimsy, support bracing of tubing or angle iron should be tack-welded in place before any cutting is done. This is critical of the back window area when this area is going to be cut from the top for re-slanting. Check the accompanying photos for an idea of this type of bracing.

Mark the A-B-C post areas where the cuts will be made. On the door posts this is usually very simple, and the windshield posts are usually cut with the midpoint of the windshield width (as seen from straight head-on) as the middle of the cut. This way the two areas align when the section is removed. At the C-post area, things get different.

If there is enough area beneath the rear window and main body, this can be the section removed to compensate for the chop,

leaving the rear window with a stock slant. Refer to the accompanying drawings to get an idea what happens here. If the rear window is to be slanted, metal to the window sides may also need to be removed/added. If the rear window is very large, it may be necessary to recess the rear glass area into the body. It is in this area where many amateurs get lost on a top chop And it is here where many top chops lose the flow of the top into the deck lid area. Fortunately, if the first attempt. Just seems to look awkward, the entire metal can be cut apart and redone. This is where the patience part comes in.

Cutting the top apart can be done with a variety of tools. The door post/windshield post areas can be cut with a hacksaw or a power saw. A power hacksaw works well, even a carpenter's electric saw with a carbide blade can be used. WEAR EYE GOGGLES! The new plasma cutters are also used. Just be sure to make all cuts "square" to each other for future alignment.

Cut the top marks first. This will leave the section to be removed attached to the body, which is far more rigid. Once the top section is lifted clear of the car, the remaining cuts are made. Save all the sections that are to be removed, as you may use various parts again.

Generally, the body area is strong enough not to need crossbracing when the top is severed, and only a very few tops need bracing. This assumes the body is attached to a frame. If not, brace the body.

If the cuts have been made parallel, they should realign. Here, the assumption is that the windshield posts will be aligned at the stock angle. Lower the top section until the posts align, and tack weld. Measure the windshield opening very carefully. Both sides of the opening should be the same. If not, break a tack weld on one side and work the cut area down. With the A-posts aligned, the B-posts should be out of alignment, the top section being well ahead of the lower section. At the C-post area there should be a large gap between the area beneath the rear window and the deck lid area.

It should be noted that a top can be chopped more in front than in back, and vice-versa. If this is the case, the B-post area will be where some extra work is needed to get the exact gap.

Before going further, check the cutdown windshield for correct fit. Do it now, while things are just tack-welded, because it is almost a certainty that the one-piece type windshield will not fit.the opening precisely. Cut the windshield and bend the windshield opening lip to fit the glass, otherwise it is probable that the windshield will be broken trying to make it fit an improper opening. This is not as much a problem with older cars having flat, two-piece windshields. If the windshield is going to be a glue-in flush fit, the final fitting of the metal can wait. If the windshield is not going to be cut, but will be recessed down into the firewall area, all this work should be done before final fitting of the glass, also to prevent breaking the glass.

Once the exact roofline slope has been determined and the top is tack-welded at windshield posts and somewhere around the quarter panel area, the door posts can be cut and fit. Since the alignment was done by sliding the top forward to the windshield posts, the door posts must be slanted to fit. On some GM products the posts were already slanted, on most Ford products the door posts were vertical. The photos show how this is done.

The area around the rear window may or may not be slanted, depending upon how the rear window will look if it is changed from the stock slope. Some builders of 1949-53 Mercurys, for example, leave the rear window slant as original, and fill in the gap between rear window and deck lid. Others contend this makes the car look too much like a Hudson, and they cut a lot of slices in the metal around the rear window to lay it down. Again, check the photos to see how this is accomplished.

And, there are some builders who will cut the top apart from side to side and align the windshield and rear window locations. This effectively separates the top, requiring the addition of a band of metal to make up the gap. On some cars of the later

1960s, the top support posts curve inward, as seen from the front. This means the top does not align fore/aft as well as side/side. In this case, the top is cut into quarters so all the posts can be aligned, then inserts are added from side to side and front to back. More complicated, but usually necessary. Most builders go ahead and mark the doors at the same time they mark the posts, but they often do not chop the door window area until after the top is tack-welded back to the body. When the door tops are cut apart, the same kind of misalignment problems exist as with the top, but if the builder very carefully inspects the window area, it can be determined that part of the section to be removed can be welded back into the structure where needed to make it longer.

Garnish moldings are rapidly disappearing from modern customs, as builders learn how to use upholstery to cover the area (as with new cars). But if the garnish molding is to be used, it is cut apart the same way the door window area is modified, and pieced back together. Use care when deciding where to make the cuts and the moldings can be reattached using the same screw holes.

When welding the top back in place, it is highly recommended that a MIG welder be used. These are the new wire-feed shielded arc type welders, and even the smaller household current 110 units work well with sheet metal. These are called "cold" welders, because the concentrate the welding heat so well, causing very minimal distortion. The weld beads aren't very pretty, but the weld is ground smoothed anyway. It is possible to rent these machines, so a purchase is not always necessary (although it is recommended).

Try to work the metal as smooth as possible before adding any filler. As mentioned elsewhere in this book, consider covering the bare metal with a good etching two-part primer (very thin coat) before adding any filler. And keep the amount of filler used very small. You want only a thin coat, not a great gob. Finish all the welded beads, everywhere, for a professional appearance.

Any chrome or stainless trim around glass can be cut apart and welded, then replated. The rubber glass gaskets can be cut apart, and glued together with black silicon cement. This is really the place to take time and do a good job, because crummy work here makes a great piece of top chopping look shabby.

As we've said, the same procedures apply to nearly every car, be it a sedan or a coupe, no matter the make. But there will be minor differences in fitting the metal back together, this is where the builder must start to use some imagination. Anyone can chop a top, and everyone can make mistakes. But mistakes can be remedied. Planning and patience are the most vital ingredients of this part of customizing.

Merc windshield posts are aligned after section is removed, slices in corners (arrows) allow sideways alignment. Drawing shows where rear window area is usually cut away on wraparound rear windows.

Cut
Here

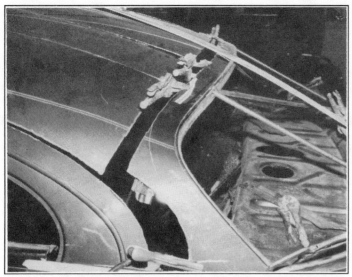

Above - Braces are tack welded in rear window opening before any cutting is done, the gap shown results from moving top forward to align at windshield posts. Long piece of metal follows window and roof line to get that right, arrows show where roof metal is sliced lengthwise to get the contour smooth. Dick Dean method.

Below - Gene Winfield method includes wide band insert above Merc rear window, in this case the sedan is being turned into a hardtop so a section of metal is welded to the quarter panel and a side window channel is welded in to serve as glass guide and top support.

Chopping Convertibles

Chopping a convertible is actually more difficult that chopping a sedan. When the windshield posts are cut down, the distance the top must span is actually longer than original. If the top mechanism is lengthened accordingly, the mechanism will usually no longer operate properly. It is possible to relocate the swivel point of the top assembly, but this is all a pure trial and error situation, usually done with the side windows in a down position. Once such a folding top is mounted to work, the door window area (usually including vent windows) must be cutdown. Then the quarter windows must be reshaped to fit the new top contour. If all this is done carefully, the door windows need not be cut, they simply don't roll up as far. However, and this is important, the window mechanism is designed to "load" the system when the window is all the way up, so it may be necessary to tinker with this mechanism a bit to keep the not-all-the-way-up window from gradually working its way down when the car is driven. Usually not a problem with power windows.

When the convert is chopped the top line is changed at the rear bow, as well, which means the area between where the top enters the body cavity and the deck lid might have to be reworked.

A trick set-up recently noted is the use of a pre 1975 GM entire folding top mechanism on a 1949-53 Mercury. Here the top was just the correct height to work with a chopped windshield, and did all the necessary folding. The same idea should work on all of the "long" converts. It might be that some of the folding......tops from compact cars of the early 1960s would also work on smaller older convertibles. Worth some investigation.

Right - The classic Mercury profile is very difficult to beat because the rest of the car's lines fit a top chop so very well. This is an excellent example of the one-third (top) to two-thirds (body) rule.

Below - Look very closely at GM product tops of the 1949 and later variety and note they are very similar to 1955 and later types, in this case the top is aligned at the windshield posts, side posts slanted, rear window moved forward.

The 1955-57 Chevy has a wraparound windshield, so the windshield posts are the point for alignment. Typically these cars are only chopped from 2 to 3 inches, cutting the front and rear glass is difficult and should be left to an experienced professional. This is a hardtop, so the only top support is at windshield and where top meets quarter panel.

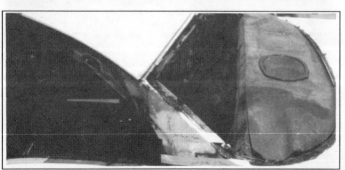

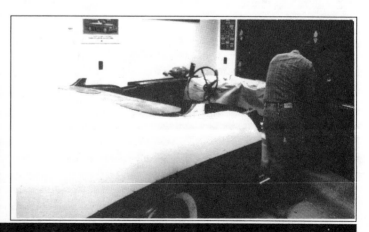

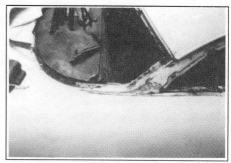

Above - This series shows how quarter post moves forward after chopping, package tray area can be moved forward so stock slant to window is achieved.

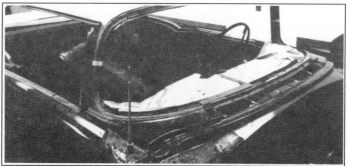

Windshield posts do not align perfectly sideways so cuts must be made at bottom of post and apex of top curve. Arrows show where the door post and vent window are cut during initial fitting phase.

Original top trim is sliced apart at the quarter area in same location as top metal, pieces are welded back together (very careful here) and then refinished. These types of chops are usually more difficult that an older cars.

Jim Baker took series of pix when his '47 Mercury was chopped by David Guymon at Precision Paint and Body in Denison, Texas. In this case the door posts were aligned and windshield posts slanted, rear window was cut out and slanted. Cutting the top on Ford products from 1935 through 1948 is very similar, GM products vary only in the door post area, so what applies to one chop usually applies to many others.

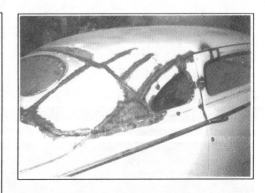

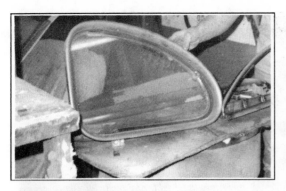

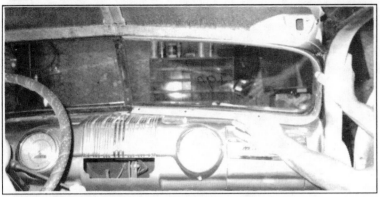

Garnish moldings are easy to reshape, do some planning and it gets even easier. On the door window frame, pieces taken from cuts front and rear (arrows) were used as inserts on top section which had to be lengthened. Sometimes, pieces are traded side for side.

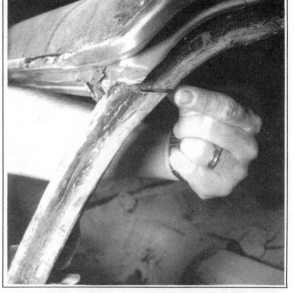

Finger points to area of windshield post on car with radical shape shield, always shape posts on such a car to fit the glass. On some late models, it is necessary to cut the top into quarter sections so everything will fit fore/aft and side/side.

When the top is chopped, requiring a lower-profile windshield, one technique is to recess the windshield into the cowl. To do this, the cowl is modified to permit the windshield to be positioned lower without the necessity of cutting the glass. In this case, the cowl has been dished to allow the installation of hidden windshield wipers, similar to many current-model cars. The reverse side of the lower part of the windshield is sealed to the cowl.

W hen chopping a top, one of the complexities is making windshield, backlight and side window glass fit the new profile. There are a couple of methods of making stock glass fit a chopped vehicle. Putting the glass is an obvious solution, but there is always the risk of breakage, and unless you have an extensive supply of replacement glass you may prefer to look for another alternative. That alternative is called recessing.

Recessing Glass

Depending upon the nature of the custom work being done to the top, it is sometimes possible to recess the glass into the body. Basically, recessing is just lowering the bottom edge of the glass into whatever part of the body is beneath it.

In the case of a windshield, the lower edge of the glass is recessed into the cowl. Modern automobiles with hidden windshield wiper systems make use of a recessed windshield to serve as the resting surface for the w`ipers when they are down in their hiding position. The bottom part of the windshield extends below the level of the hood into a dished out area occupied by the wiper mechanisms.

The backlight can be recessed into the trunk by simply opening up a slot in the rear deck beneath the glass and allowing it to protrude into the trunk cavity. To do this, the entire lower backlight frame is severed from the rear deck and the whole thing is lowered into the trunk cavity. This way, the glass is still supported by the stock gasket and frame around its entire circumference.

Of course, then you need to close up the slot and seal the space where the glass goes through the sheetmetal so moisture won't sneak into the trunk that way.

As long as the body and doors haven't been sectioned, the side windows can remain stock depth and simply not be rolled up all the way. That's the quick and easy way to recess side window glass.

Cutting Flat Glass

It isn't too difficult to make your own window replacements when working with flat glass. Such things as quarter windows are fairly easy to make if you know the techniques and work carefully.

The tools necessary for cutting flat glass include the following:
1. grease pencil
2. glass cutter
3. razor blade
4. lighter fluid
5. flat working table

It's not a bad idea to include a set of safety glasses in that list, and perhaps a pair of gloves, and use them whenever working on glass.

Follow along with this series of photos to see how it's done.

Start by using a grease pencil to draw the outline of the size and shape of glass that you need cut from the larger piece. Then, carefully and precisely follow the outline with a glass cutter to scribe a groove around the entire perimeter.

Left - Scribe the reverse side of the glass as well, being careful to follow exactly the outline scribed on the top side.

Below Left - Gently break the glass along the straight edge of the cut by working it up and down until it snaps. Then, use a razor to cut through the safety-glass lamination and remove the discard piece.

Below Right - An alternate method is to burn through the plastic lamination layer. After breaking the glass by working it (gently) up and down, fill the split with lighter fluid and ignite it.

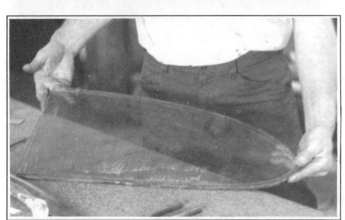

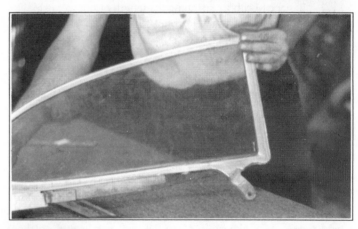

Above Left -After a little practice , it doesnt take long to cut a nice new quarter window using these techniques. If desired, you can finish the edge of the glass by touching it to a belt grinder, but this step is optional.

Above Right - The final step is to install the glass in the gasket and frame, then it's ready to go back in the car.

Left - For a custom touch, the glass can be etched with a graphic patern. This can be done either before or after final installation.

Sandblasting Windshields

Most professionals can cut flat glass without too much trouble, but cutting curved glass is art, mixed with science, mixed with luck. It is possible to cut curved glass, such as a windshield in the traditional manner, but the risk of breakage is very high. That's why the sandblast method has become so popular. Tom Durocher, owner of Thomas' in Pontiac, Michigan has all the tricks down pat, and demonstrates here how the sandblast technique works.

To begin with, if the windshield you're cutting happens to be your first attempt, make sure you have access to a ready supply of windshields, because even with the relatively safe sandblast method more than likely you're going to need them after you break the first one. This is tricky stuff, and even experienced glass cutters can ruin a windshield.

The tools necessary for cutting a windshield or backlight include the following:

1. a white grease pencil
2. 1/2-inch masking tape
3. tape measure
4. glass cutter
5. sand blaster
6. single edge razor blade
7. a piece of rubber stripping the length of the \windshield and 2 inches wide
8. 2-inch masking tape
9. heavy cardboard (enough to cover the entire wind shield)
10. safety glasses
11. a glass grinder
12. a windshield support stand (U-shaped stand with adjustable center support)
13. propane torch
14. can of satin finish trim black

With all the tools and supplies assembled, you can start to work. The first step is to mark the cutting line. Begin by removing any old remaining butyl, urethane and other debris from the windshield pinch weld. Carefully place the new windshield on the glass stops located on the cowl. Working from left to right with the white grease pencil, mark (on the inside) with a broken line where the top line of the windshield should be. Now, using the tape measure, keep a uniform distance from the top edge of the windshield and mark the outside of the windshield with the grease pencil. Next, run 1/2-inch masking tape along the line you just finished marking on the outside of the windshield, making sure you adhere closely to the line marked. This will eventually be the cut-indicating line.

Step two is to prepare for sandblasting. Remove the windshield from the vehicle and carefully place it on the support stand with the inside facing up. Run 2-inch masking tape along the taped line on the exterior of the windshield, being careful to follow that line exactly. Place the rubber strip along the tape edge (inside) and tape it in place, leaving the top edge of the rubber exposed. Place your patterned cardboard over the rubber strip, staying approximately 1/4-inch from the edge of the rubber. Tape it in place.

Step three is sandblasting. Remove the windshield and support stand to an area safe for sandblasting. Making sure your safety glasses are in place, begin sandblasting by directing the sand at the edge of the rubber. Continue to attack this line until the plastic lamination between the two layers of glass is exposed along the entire length of the windshield. Taking the razor blade, carefully cut through the exposed plastic lamination, and remove it from the entire length of the windshield.

Step four involves cutting the remaining glass. Place the windshield and support stand on a strong table.Thoroughly clean the now-exposed outside layer of glass. With steady and even pressure, carefully make your cut with the glass cutter, starting at one edge and continuing without stopping or hesitating to the opposite edge. You cannot successfully go back over this cut if it is not done correctly the first time. With the non-cutting edge of the glass cutter, carefully tap along the entire line from the underside of the cut. You will be able to see the glass "run" along the cut edge. After you have completed the "run," firmly grasp the edge to be removed and break the line by applying downward pressure to the edge of the windshield.

Now you will need to cut the corners to the original shape of the curve to obtain the proper fit. Doing one side at a time, carefully mark the cutting line. With the glass cutter, cut along the marked line. Make a "run" in the glass using the same method as before. Turn the windshield over and cut along the same line. This cut must be made exactly over the cut on the reverse side. Again, make the "run". Using rubber-coated grips, firmly grasp the piece to be removed and heat the cut with a propane torch. Continue heating until you can work the piece to be removed just enough so that you can get a single-edge razor blade in between the glass. Cut through the lamination. Repeat these steps on the opposite side.

Step five is finishing the glass. With the glass grinder, grind down the cut edge until there is a smooth finished edge. Test fit the windshield to the vehicle and make any necessary grinding adjustments. If there is black trim on the windshield edge, tape off the cut edges and lightly sandblast the area to be painted black. Complete the edge by painting, using a satin finish trim black.

The final step is to install the windshield. Prime the windshield channel with a pinch weld primer. Run a bead of urethane in the channel and put the windshield in place, making sure that it is resting properly on the windshield supports. Reinstall any windshield trim. it will take approximately 24 hours for the urethane to cure.

Using a white grease pencil and tape measure, carefully mark the cutting line on the upper part of the windshield. Mark first on the inside of the glass, following the contour of the roofline, then transfer the line to the exterior surface of the glass, using a tape measure to maintain a constant distance from the edge.

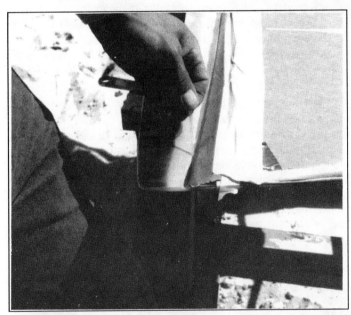

Left - After masking off the windshield to protect it, sandblast along the marked line. When the layer of glass has been blasted all the way through to the plastic lamination, take the razor blade and cut through the lamination. Then remove it along the entire length of the windshield.

Below Left - After removing the unneeded portion of the windshield, the cut edge is smoothed on a glass grinder. After finishing the edge, make a trial fit of the windshield and make any necessary grinding adjustments until the fit is perfect. Then install the windshield.

Below Right - On the reverse side of the windshield, use the glass cutter to scribe a cut line exactly following the sandblasted line on the opposite side. This cut must be made with consistent pressure and without hesitation along the entire length of the windshield.

ELECTRICS

When someone talks about custom car electrics, the subject is almost never about ignition or lighting or gauges. The subject is about electric doors, and electric deck lid latches, and esoteric matter that most of hot rodding never has a concern with. All of this because the customizer likes to remove the outside door handles and deck lid release. And nowdays, to have electric windows.

Early on, customizers would use the GM starter solenoid as the prime mover for any latch mechanism. This solenoid had a lot of linear travel, and a lot of power, important when trying to overcome the strength of door latch springs. Most of these solenoids (early on) were 6-volt.

In recent years, other makes of solenoids have been used, and the position of the solenoids has been changed. When there is a clearance problem in the door housing, the solenoid can be positioned out of harm's way, connecting to the door latch via a cable and sliding glass (household type) rollers. Smaller diameter solenoids have been introduced to the aftermarket, such as those from Mr. Gasket company. These have plenty of strength for the trunk latch, but they sometimes lack enough power to overcome the door latch spring. The small electric screw motors from Ball's Hot Rod Parts overcome lots of the solenoid shortcomings, probably setting the scene for many years to come.

Relays are needed in these systems, we include information about that subject. Switches are also needed, we leave them up to you. Switches of many varieties are used, just get items that are heavy duty. Mount these switches where they aren't likely to get wet, especially the outside units. It may be cool to have the outside door switch under the rocker panel, but that's a great place for water and corrosion to kill the switch. Or cause it to short. Some customizers have used high-tech proximity switches for the doors, neat to impress the guys but sometimes the cause of many troubles. Recently, special entry cards have been devised for the switch, in this case you probably need to call on an electronics expert for guidance.

Electric windows are all the rage now. You can modify late model electric window lifts to work with the early windows, but if a single lift arm is used you may have to keep experimenting with the motor location until you get glass movement without bind. Some aftermarket window lifts are available that work in a pure vertical fashion, others have the more traditional arm. Really cool is the idea we picked up at Gene Winfield's shop (but an idea that is being used all across the nation, on both rods and customs), where the entire door inner structure, including power lift mechanism, from a late model car door is cut out and grafted to the early car door electrics.

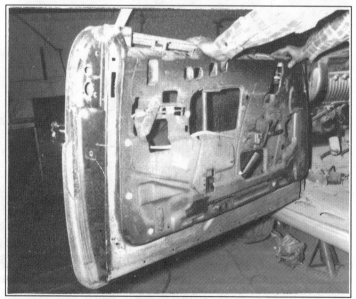

Door of this Mercury has had the inner structure cut away, with just enough of the lip left to maintain rigidity while working with new insert.

The inner panel from a late 1970s or 1980s GM car door is cut and trimmed until it will just fit the Mercury door. Select donor units that are nearly the same size as the Mercury door. Guide rod for late model curved glass must be replaced with a straight guide (homemade) that will locate the early car flat glass.

 # Relays

by Skip Readio

When supplying current to some of the more demanding circuits in a modern car, manufacturers resort to relays. A typical, all-around, relay is the GM air conditioning relay. It can be purchased through a number of sources, either from a GM dealer under the part number 1115858 or from auto parts stores under the following part numbers: FILKO RL-11, NAPA RY-124, STANDARD RY-12.

The connectors on a GM air conditioning relay look like this:

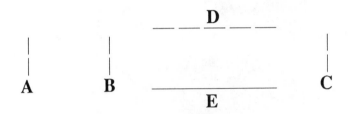

The two horizontal lugs (D & E) go to the relay's coil, so they can be connected up either way (ground on top, switch on bottom or visa-versa, it makes no difference)

The right hand vertical lug (C) is the input, the left hand lug (A) is the normally-open output. The second from the left (B) is the normally-closed lug. When the relay is "at rest" the current path is from the right lug (C) to the second from the left (B).

When the relay is energized (you want to turn on the device) the current path is from the right lug (C) to the left lug (A).

Installation Instructions

For ALL applications, regardless of whether you want to use your ignition switch to enable the relay or not, connect a circuit breaker to the right lug (C) and the other side of the circuit breaker to the battery (straight to the battery). The rating on the circuit breaker will depend on the current requirements of the device you want to actuate. Most devices you will want to operate will require at least a 25 amp circuit breaker.

Connect the left lug (A) to the device you want to operate, such as:
    the electric cooling fan (when activated by the AC system)
    or the air conditioner compressor clutch.
    or the power window switches
    or the door latch solenoids
    or the trunk solenoids
    etc.,

Connecting the ACTIVATE Circuit

For power windows and power seats (devices you want to work only when the key in ON or in the ACCessory position):

Connect one of the horizontal lugs (D) to ground and connect the other one (E) to the ACC post on your ignition switch. This will energize the relay and provide power to the switches for the devices you want to operate such as power windows and power seats ONLY when the key is in the ACCessory or the RUN positions.

For air conditioner compressors clutches, electric fans, door latch solenoids, trunk solenoids:

Connect one of the horizontal lugs (E) to the switch (air conditioning compressor switch/remote cooling fan switch, solenoid actuating button, etc.). Connect the other post (D) to ground. This will allow you to actuate the device regardless of whether the key is in the ignition or not.

In the case of the air conditioner compressor and auxiliary fan control, the power to actuate the switch will come off the RUN side of the ignition switch so even though there is power to the relay, there won't be power to the switch to activate the relay. You won't have to worry about leaving the air conditioner on because lug (E) won't have voltage on it once the key is turned off and the relay will de-activate.

For trunk and door solenoids, connect a wire from the battery to the solenoid-activating switch and then from the switch, connect a second wire to the relay lug (E). The switch will only be required to carry very low current so a 5 amp fuse in the supply line should work fine. Put the fuse as close to the supply voltage (battery) as possible to protect the entire switch circuit.

If you have one of those outside-the-car remote controls for your power windows, then you won't need to shut off current to the switches. If you did, you won't be able to get your power windows to work with the car locked up and that's what most builders have in mind when ordering these kits. The kit allows the owner to roll down the window from outside the car and reach in and open the door, thus eliminating the need for latch solenoids. It means that ONLY the power window power supplying wires need be run through the door pillar instead of both latch solenoid wires and window activating wires. It is possible to put the window's remote control box on the battery-side of a power window relay but to do so means you'll have to run ANOTHER heavy gauge wire into the door from the pillar for every window you want to operate that way. Outside-remote control windows means that, unless you want to run a lot more wires through the door pillar, the windows will work whether the ignition switch is on or not.

Don't forget, if you're using a battery kill switch you're going to have to bypass if if you want to be able to get into your car. If you don't, the relays won't work once you flip the kill switch. Connect your circuit breakers to the battery side of the kill switch for any device that MUST operate whether the kill switch is ON or OFF. (That goes for clocks and digital-tuning radio memories as well

Screwmotors

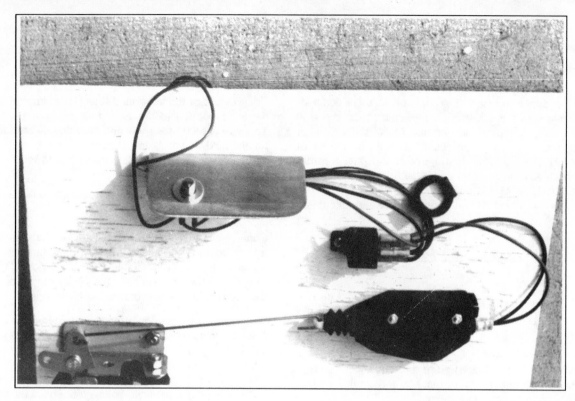

A really trick item now available is the screwmotor from Ball's Hot Rod Parts. Installation depends upon whether the unit is being put in a fiberglass or a steel body.

For 'glass cars, cut a hole in the inner door panel which is the profile of the screwmotor. Make up a mounting plate of steel, aluminum, or plastic that is larger than the screw motor. Mount the motor inside the profile cutout, with the mounting plate on the outside. This plate attaches to the door structure. The pull pin on the screwmotor should be on a straight line with the latch trip lever. A linkage wire (heavy welding rod is about right diameter) is cut about 1 1/2 inches longer so the ends can be bent into closed loops. When this linkage is attached to latch and motor, there should be about a quarter-inch of free travel.

Wire leads for the screwmotor are 12-volt and ground, and may be activated by pushbuttons, micro switches, or remote controls. The motor will push or pull, depending on position of the 12-volt and ground wires. On steel bodies, the motor is grounded automatically, on 'glass cars you need to run a ground from the motor to a ground terminal. The screwmotor has a power rating of 35 Newtons, and can be used on trunks, hoods, doors, gas filler doors, etc. Motors are watertight and have 3/4-inch travel. They are as fast as a solenoid.

Options

Whether you go with starter solenoids, or the Ball's screwmotor, you need to know that there may be other options available. In the first place, you may not want to have an electric motor for the door or deck lid latch at all. It is possible to use some of the currently available "blacked out" door handles. It may also be possible to build a recess into the body just adjacent to the door/deck latch and use a couple of fingers inserted into this recess to operate the latch.

The door lock motors on some new cars are quite strong and will sometimes be powerful enough for doors. Again, the newer cars have less power requirement than the older cars for the door latches, so your options are varied.

Another trick that has been used effectively in the past is to actuate the doors/deck with a special "key", said key actually being a length of heavy wire. In one case, the wire is used to jimmy the door lock or windwing handle (ala breaking-and-entering), in another (as with the deck lid), the wire exits through the body in an inconspicuous place and is attached directly to the latch.

Finally, there is the credit card type of lock that some of the electronic wizards are beginning to use. In at least one case known to the author, all the little holes in the card did nothing . . . the front edge of the plastic card simply touched the electric switch!

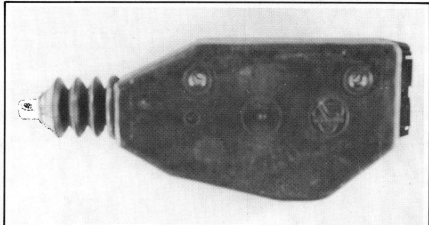

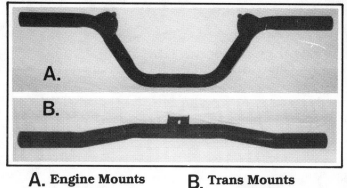

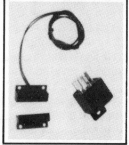

Headlights

photos courtesy Cris Boggess, Gene Winfield,
Gerry Charvat, Bill's Custom Louvering

While the grille area sets much of the theme for any custom car, the head and tail lights add a great deal of the overall vehicle styling character. Perhaps this is because, like bumpers, the lights are necessary evils that simply must be included. Therefore, might as well work with them and integrate them into the overall design. Granted, this is also the area where many builders, pro and amateur alike, get into major design problems. What seems like a great idea simple doesn't work. If someone with a drawing talent can make a few sketches before the work is done, such ideas might never come to be. The exersize here is to show how some of the more common light treatments are handled, but since each custom is different, all these ideas are simply...ideas.

The rounded fenders seem to accept flush frenched headlights very well, in this cast of the Mercury at right, the grille surround is also flushed off as a complement. The Ford on the opposite page uses tunneled lights with inset rings, and the Mercury below includes the stock visor lights.

TRICK BUCKET STUFF

Thanks to the two-piece headlight rim frenching kits from Night Prowlers company, it is possible to leave the headlight bucket in stock location. This makes lamp adjustment and replacement simple, as well. Here, the outer rim (headlamp door) is bonded to the fender, and the inner ring can be held in place with a silicon glue. This way, the ring is solid, but can be pried loose for lamp replacement or adjustment. The headlight bucket is left in stock location. This silicon glue trick can be used in many other places on a custom.

Frenching

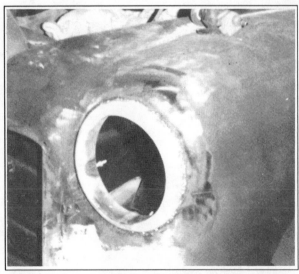

Headlight rings are welded to the fender, look closely at the right photo and note studs welded to rear of rings so headlight buckets can be inserted from rear.

Frenched headlights seems to be one of the immediate distinctions of many custom built cars, and it is a practice that really does lead directly to France. Early on, French designers learned the fact that a headlight that seemed to be a smooth transition from the body was less disruptive to the design. But such a design feature requires additional production effort and cost, so it simply isn't much of a production car feature. Until recently, however, as the new streamlined car bodies start to utilize shaped headlights.

Early on, American customizers included frenched headlights, and the effect is stunning. The culprit to design flow is the headlamp door, or rim. If this rim can be smoothed into the surrounding panel, it seems to make a dramatic difference in appearance. Many early model customs (body styles produced prior to 1949) will often include frenched lights, it is almost an axiom that custom styles between 1949-1954 will use the true frenched light. But, after 1954, the full and semi-tunnelled frenched light appears, in all body styles of all years. Confusing?

The pure frenched headlight is one that has the surrounding metal sweep directly to the sealed beam light unit, and there may or may not be a small chrome rim visible around the sealed beam. During the mid-Fifties production cars began to use headlamp doors that included a set-back inner chrome rim, from 1/2 to 1-inch in depth. Custom builders immediately seized upon this ring and used it with the frenched fender, giving a different appearance. A kind of minor tunneled look. So, from a purely nostalgia standpoint, any headlight treatment with such an inner ring would mean a building era after 1954. In the true tunneled treatment, there may or may not be an inner plated rim, and this rim might have been custom made. As another rule of thumb, the fully tunneled headlight will be set back into the fender an inch or more.

Early on, any headlight frenching treatment led directly to a major problem -- headlight bucket adjustment. The reason the factory has a headlamp rim is ease of light replacement and adjustment. The headlight opening in the fender receives a separate "bucket", and into this bucket sets the headlamp. The bucket is held to the fender opening with clips or bolts, and the headlamp is held to the bucket with adjustment screws/bolts. If the headlight rim is going to be welded to the fender, some kind of headlamp replacement/adjustment procedure must be included.

The direct approach is to simply mount the headlamp bucket from the backside of the fender. In this way, the assembly can be approached for service from underneath the fender, but it is clumsy at best, requiring that the entire bucket be removed every time an adjustment is made, and then adjustment is by trial and error. A tedious job, so some customizers made extra effort so that adjustment bolts were reversed and reachable from the rear.

When the inner chrome ring is included, it is possible to reach the adjustment bolts, therefore the bucket can be installed from the rear and the adjustment/replacement can be made from the front (when the chrome rim is removed). There are variations on this theme, of course, but this is the basic element of frenched headlights.

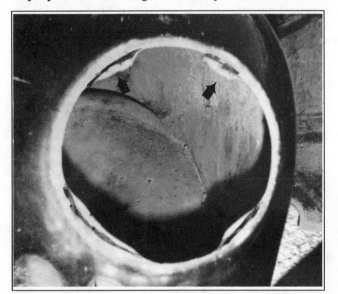

Typical frenching procedure starts by removing the headlight bucket and trimming the opening edges (arrows.) From here on it is a matter of deciding what kind of headlight treatment will be used. The more traditional frenching as shown at the start of this section can even be done without all the trimming, here the fender is being readied to accept the Chrysler round headlight rim of recent years.

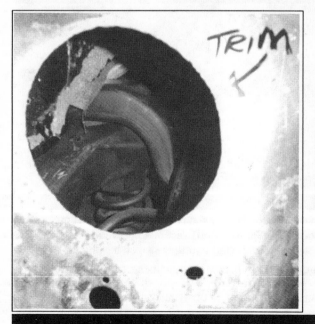

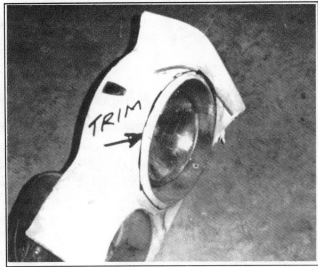

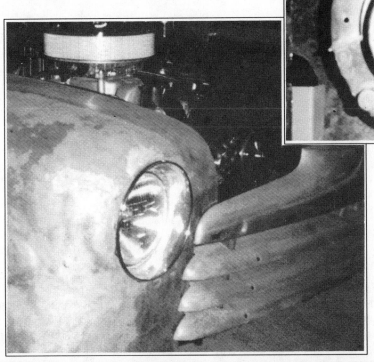

Chrysler headlight bucket sets into the fender with a very nice recessed appearance. The Cordoba units are readily available, unlike some of the older Ford items, and the assembly is fully adjustable from the front side.

Taillights

photos courtesy Gene Winfield,
Mark Williams, Jeff Soper, John Lee

As with the headlights, the taillights are a definite mark of the custom car. Sometimes, however, taillights are changed without enough thought given design compatibility with the body style. The result can be a major disappointment, therefore more than casual planning is needed when working on any taillight treatment.

Custom taillights usually fall into two categories: Modified and stock, Custom taillights us will include a stock bezel (rim), frenching, and/or tunneling.

Modified taillights may come from modified stock units, or from taillight lens made from scratch. If a unit is scratchbuilt, it is imperative that the diffuser insert be included. That is, the backside of a factory lens will have a pattern of sharp pointed pyramids which will cause the bulb light to defuse much better. This must be included in any scratchbuilt unit. Most often, the customizer will use the clear defuser panel from something like a fluorescent light fixture, cut and shaped to fit behind the custom lens.

Custom lens can be shaped over a wood mold, merely lay plastic on the "buck" and heat in an oven until the plastic sags over the mold. The diffuser will shape in the same way. Leave the room doors open when using plastic in an oven, to clear fumes.

Trick: To restore an old, cracked and discolored lens, or to color a clear lens, it is possible to use a red tinting paint (such as used to make Candy Apple). Apply in a very thin coat. Works great. Obviously, this is applied to the inside of the lens.

When using a stock taillight lens, it is easier to include the original taillight bucket. But a custom bucket can be made up from sheet stock. To make the lights brighter, either paint the bucket with white or silver paint, have it chrome plated, or install some wrinkled aluminum foil against the bucket face.

Sometimes, it is desirable to actually include a section of the donor car fender when using a factory taillight.

The main problem of frenching a taillight is attachment of the lens to the bucket. As mentioned with the headlight section, don"t overlook the use of silicon glue. This serves to seal the light bucket from moisture and dust as well as hold the lens in place.

And sometimes, the taillight from a donor car just doesn't seem to look right, although there seems to be a good design involved. In this case, it might be that the donor taillight requires the original design bumper so that the entire design effect is attained. It is all a matter of careful planning. The execution part is easy (usually!!).

Custom taillight treatments are many and varied, each depending upon the design instincts of the owner/builder. That being the case, there is ample opportunity to come up with incompatible taillight designs for a particular car. A lot of study and forethought needs to be given before completing this area of the car.

Ranging from subtle to wild, modified taillights are one of the marks of a custom car. Taillight assemblies can be borrowed from other cars, or in some cases completely custom built.

Custom Lights

Sometimes, a very specific design can be achieved by including custom lights, a design that really sets the car apart. Such is the case of this slant-eye taillight treatment by Gene Winfield several years ago on a shoebox Ford.

Here, the taillights flow into a cross-body treatment of the decklid, and the effect is very unusual. Note that the decklid corners were modified, as well.

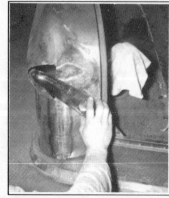

No one following this shoebox Ford could help but look at least twice at the custom taillight arrangement fabricated by Gene Winfield. Integrated into the treatment is a modified decklid that ties everything together.

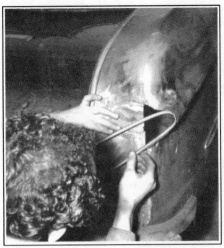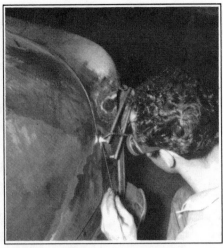

After playing with lens positions until a decision was made, round stock was bent, welded in place on the rear of the fenders and molded in to form the taillight surround.

Following the angle established by the taillights, the decklid was marked and cut across the corners. The small triangular piece that was removed from the lid was welded to the adjacent corner.

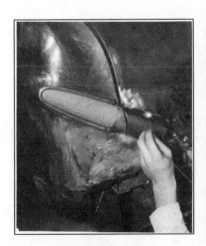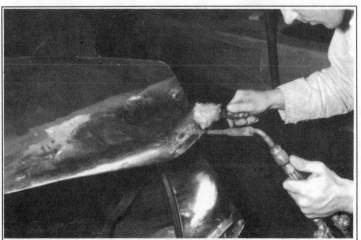

To carry the flow of the slanted taillights across the bottom of the decklid, sheetmetal was shaped to conform with the contour of the taillights and then welded in place. To finish off the installation, the seams are leaded.

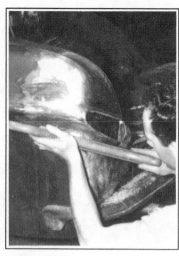

To acheive a perfect finish contour on the taillight surround and decklid, a combination of wire brush and a couple of different lead files are employed.

Trading Lights

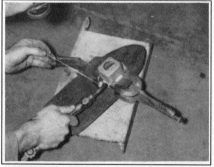

Using the back of the '56 Lincoln taillight as a template, a pattern is drawn for making the backing plate/lamp support.

After cutting the backing plate out of sheetmetal, the lamp box is tacked in place.

Below - A piece of cardboard is used as a template for forming the fender extension which will house the taillight. This pattern is then transferred to sheetmetal.

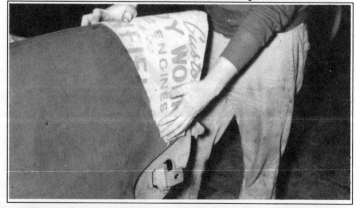

There are several "stock"factory taillights that seem to have heavy favor with customizers through the years. The fin-era Chrysler lights and the Packard fin lights come to mind. This example from Winfield is of another favorite, the Lincoln assembly. As mentioned, the light seems to look best when combined with the Lincoln bumper, so follow along as we see how Winfield installed a 1956 Lincoln taillight duo and bumper on a 1951 Chevrolet.

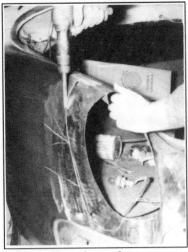

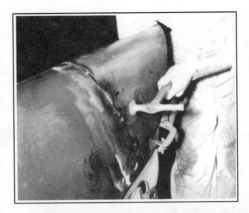

The cardboard template was used to mark the stock '51 Chevy rear fender for making the cut. In this case, a pneumatic chisel is used to sever the unneeded sheetmetal.

Top Center - The sheetmetal extension, patterned after the cardboard template, is welded in place.

Top Right - The lens retainer is made to fit just inside the rear edge of the taillight opening in the fender.

Near Right - A lip for the taillight opening is made of round stock to create a rolled edge at the rear of the sheetmetal.

Far Right - Lincoln rear bumper had to be narrowed to fit the width of the '51 Chevy. After cutting apart and rewelding, the bumper was sent to the chrome shop for plating.

Near Right In the highest order of bodywork, the weld seams on the fender extensions are filled with lead.

Far Right - Lincoln rear bumper had to be narrowed to fit the width of the '51 Chevy. After cutting apart and rewelding, the bumper was sent to the chrome shop for plating.

Bottom - The finished product is distinctly custom with semi-fin rear fenders, Lincoln taillights and bumper and a few other tricks thrown in for good measure.

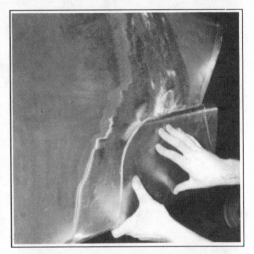

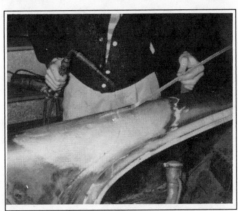

Third Brake Lights

A small raised panel with five light sockets was built into the roof, just forward of the rear window. With the light fixtures up in the raised panel, there is no obstruction in the interior and everything is easily hidden by the headliner. A rear-facing, gently rising scoop lifts from the contour of the roof just enough to cover the 3rd brakelight panel.

Photos by Jeff Soper

Although 3rd brake lights have appeared through the years on customs, this has been a very rare occurance. But now, with the new emphasis on safety, such lights can become a part of any design without being obtrusive. Consider this case of a 1957 Plymouth (see more on this car at end of the book) that includes 3rd brake lights above the rear window, included in a roof scoop that might well have been a 1960's treatment.

GRILLES

Completely custom made, this floating grille was designed and made by Gene Winfield. It eventually ended up on his famous show custom Solar Scene.

To illustrate that nearly anything can be done in the grille department, here's a mid-Fifties Chevy truck grille that found its way into the mouth of an early-Fifties Ford sedan.

The choice is yours. Find a stock grille that will work in the grille opening of your custom, or build a grille to suit your desires. Aside from dimensional limitations, the only limits to what can be done in the grille department reside in your imagination.

Before deciding what kind of grille treatment you want, it's a good idea to look at lots of other customs, whether in person or in photographs. Sketch some of your own ideas. Visit auto salvage yards to get some close-up and personal familiarity with different grille components that may be combined and adapted to fit your custom. Inspect them closely to see what kind of attachment technique and hardware are used, and do a little figuring to determine if that method of attachment is going to work in your custom or if a different approach is going to need to be invented.

If you will be leaving the grille opening relatively stock, take some horizontal and vertical measurements and make a drawing, as close to scale as possible, depicting the grille opening. Keep this with you as you search for the grille of your dreams. One method of simplifying the decision is to take a photograph of the front of your car, then superimpose photograph cutouts of a variety of grilles. This will help answer some questions about how the car will look with a custom grille installed.

If you are going to modify the grille opening, those modifications will have to wait until after you have decided upon the shape and size of the grille. Logic dictates that the grille must be in hand before you begin to modify the opening to accommodate it. But before buying the grille and dragging it home, take measurements to ensure that the face of the car is going to be dimensionally compatible with the grille.

The sky is the limit when you start swapping grilles from one car to another, as long as you are willing to do the work necessary to make them fit. Some folks go so far as to swap the entire nose from one car to another.

Likewise, there is almost no limit to what can be done if you decide to design and build your own grille from scratch. The materials involved in custom grille construction can run the gamut from round or square tubing to bar stock to cabinet door knobs.

On the following pages, we'll cover a couple of different ways to build your own grille. One is a tube grille and the other is an egg-crate grille. Then we'll show you some great examples of custom grilles that you can use for ideas.

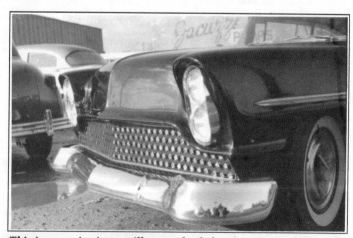

This is a very intricate grille, completely hand made. Each diamond was cut out, welded to a stud and attached to the expanded metal screen behind it, with about half an inch of standoff.

TEX SMITH'S HOTROD Mechanix

Mailed in a plain brown wrapper, so your friends and neighbors will never suspect your addiction.

1 YEAR - $24⁰⁰

NAME_____PH._____

STREET_____

CITY_____STATE_____ZIP_____

REFERRED BY _____HOMETOWN_____

MASTERCARD/VISA #_____EXP._____

SIGNED_____

CANADA AND ALL OTHER FOREIGN $28 per year (surface postage) Add $40.00 per year for first class air mail.
Payable in US funds only. Allow 6-8 weeks for first delivery.

Tex Smith Publishing 29 E. Wallace PO Box 726 Droiggs ID. 83422 (208) 354-8133

Grille Openings

A grille opening is simply a space into which a grille can be installed. Proportionally, the opening should be compatible with the intended grille so that there are no obnoxious gaps in the car's smile. This requires a bit of homework on the customizer's part, to match the opening with the selected grille, or vice-versa, to match the grille to an existing opening.

This bit of creativity can work a couple of ways. The stock opening can be filled with a stock grille from another vehicle, if the two are somewhat compatible. The stock opening can be filled with a totally custom (homebuilt) grille. The opening can be replaced by or customized to resemble the opening belonging to another vehicle, which allows a whole new batch of possibilities to be explored.

If a totally custom grille is being fitted into the opening, there are basically only two ways to make the installation work. One way is to fill the opening with the grille so that the edges can be tied into the edges of the opening in some manner with brackets. If the idea is to float a small grille in a large opening so that there is lots of space around the brightwork, some type of bracketry will need to be fabricated to support the grille without appearing to do so. This is where the height of your creative effort will come into play, designing and fabricating the whole system.

If you decide to mate an existing grille from another vehicle with the grille opening of your car, you may want to consider transferring associated parts along with the grille. Take a look at what Cris Boggess did to fit a '52 DeSoto grille in a '50 Merc grille opening. This may give you some ideas for solving your own grille/grille opening challenges.

In this case, Cris wanted to use a DeSoto grille, with its swoopy teeth that he feels were designed especially for the '50 Mercury. His solution was to use the lower pan from a 1952 or 1953 DeSoto along with the grille. In this way, the teeth fit the pan perfectly, reducing a lot of work trying to make the teeth fit the Mercury sheet metal. The result is a smooth grille opening, and this modification can be done by anyone with basic welding skills.

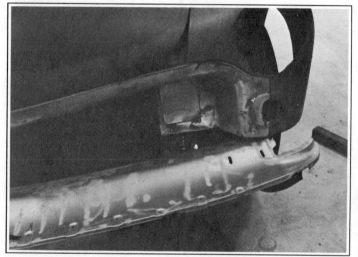

The '52 DeSoto lower grille pan is measured for fit in the Mercury. It is very close to a "drop-in" fit, with only a small amount of trimming needed at the fender attachment points. This pan can be made for fit quite a few cars of the early Fifties.

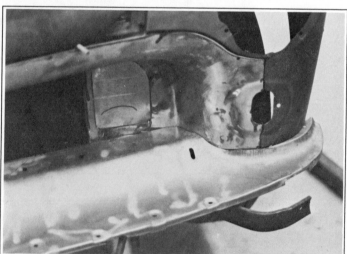

Use snips to trim the DeSoto pan until it mates with the bottom of the Mercury fenders. Don't worry about the pan edges that fail to align with the outer edges of the fenders. This will be taken care of soon.

Left - Trim the upper flange of the pan wing, then tack weld the pan to the fender and inside the grille opening.

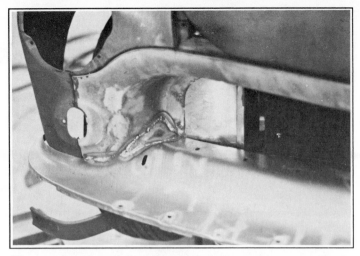

The curve portion of the cut-away DeSoto panel is reversed and makes and excellent fillet in the grille opening corner.

Note that the fender has been split at the original opening. By spreading the fender outward slightly, it will fit the pan wing nicely, otherwise the wing must be reshaped to fit the fender. Once the fender aligns with the pan outer edges, everything is welded solid.

Right - To finish off the edges of the pan where it wraps around the fenders, make up some fillets from sheet stock and weld in place.

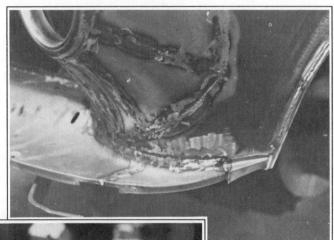

This is how the roughed-in grille opening now looks. The DeSoto grille teeth now bolt to their stock lower pan and seem to float inside the grille opening.

Custom Grille Design

Right - The grille's been around for 50 years, the car for 48, but we've never seem the harp-like '39 Buick piece in a '41 Ford before Bill Reasoner did this one recently. Housing was formed from tubing and sheetmetal to shape.

Center - 1951 Oldsmobiles came with this clean, straight bar which looks great when floated in a cavity like the '50 Merc shell molded into this '52 Ford.

Below - When Ray Goulart built this '50 Oldsmobile back in '63, he formed the oval grille opening from tubing and sheetmetal to carry out the shape of the '56 Olds top bumper bar, inverted, which serves as protection. Four chromed tube bars attach to a metal mesh that's painted flat black.

By John Lee

There seems to be a high degree of "sameness" in grille treatments appearing on custom cars these days. There's no denying that the popular units - - '51 - '53 DeSoto, '54 and '55 DeSoto, '53 and '54 Chevy, '54 Pontiac, '57 Buick and the various straight tubes - - look great, but there are others that would look as good or better - - and different - - if a little more imagination were used in designing and choosing them.

True, you don't just go down to the local junkyard and look around till you find the one you want anymore Most of the '50s cars with the grilles we loved are no longer there, or if so, the grille is bent or pitted beyond repair.

But you can still find treasures in that boneyard. The '60s and '70s cars which now populate those hallowed grounds offer all kinds of possibilities that haven't been tried yet.

Don't overlook some of the later-model plastic grilles. They're easy to alter by cutting, gluing together with epoxy and finishing with filler. With the cost of chrome plating these days, it makes sense to go for the contemporary look with a painted grille.

The examples that follow are presented to stimulate your imagination to create a new, original piece of grillework for your custom.

Al Morris frenched the stock '51 Chevy grille to the surrounding sheet metal and painted it, then inserted honeycomb-patterned plastic mesh in the slotted openings.

For this '49 Mercury, a '57 Chevy pickup oval center bar has been chromed and floated in the molded shell. A flat black mesh forms the backdrop to which round chrome drawer pulls are attached.

Butch Tucker liked the looks of the wide channel steel framework from a golf car canopy. He welded pieces together with the correct V in the middle to fit his '56 Chevy wagon's grille opening, then finished and chromed them.

Plastic PCV tubing is light and easy to work with. Bob Nordberg made up a grille from it for his late-model Chevy pickup and painted it satin black, along with the bumper and spoiler. The polished stainless border was retained for contrast.

Larry Blair made up the clean grille for his '71 Chevy pickup from 1/8" by 2" steel strap, chromed and held in place by two slotted vertical pieces of the same material.

Chrome drawer or cupboard door handles, readily available at hardware stores, make creating a novel grille design cheap and easy. Don Goodman attached a set to his '58 Ford's stock grille insert.

Above - A classic treatment for the '36 Ford is the '39 LaSalle grille, but they're almost impossible to find now. Other LaSalles plus Olds '98s and Cadillacs of the late 1930s had similar die cast pieces, but none quite so clean as this.

Above Right - Bob James mated two '61 Dodge pickup grilles together to fill the cavity of his '56 Ford pickup and painted the result body color. Fenders were angled in at the bottom to match the grille's shape.

Right - 1953 Dodge grille bar is a nice swap into a '49 - '51 Ford and provides integral directional lights. This bar also works with '52 - '54 Fords.

Below - Larry Cochran's beautiful '50 Chevy has a '50 Merc shell molded in. The rare '59 Imperial grille bar with custom-built end extensions and bullets adds visual width.

Above - The '54 Pontiac bar is a natural for the '49 - '51 Ford. When built this car, Bob Sipes molded the bar in and he painted it to match the body, leaving only the fine insert polished.

Above - Bars floating in this '59 Mercury opening are from a '56 Chrysler Windsor. The three different lengths are reversed from their order in the Chrysler housing.

Right - This sports roadster makes good use of a '51 Nash grille piece. The neat Nash units from the early 1950s have been overlooked for custom treatments.

Below - A 1955 Chrysler New Yorker bumper bar with integral directional lights had to be shortened to fit within the Mercury grille shell. It's backed with a honeycomb mesh with drawer pulls attached.

Above - Dave Losen transformed the stock grille of his '55 Ford by the addition of chrome drawer handles, an easy bolt-on operation.

Left - Another hard-to-find item is the '54 Chrysler Imperial grille, but the custom effect is worth the search. To install it in Ed Guffy's '50 Ford, Doug Thompson retained the stock directional lights and made extensions out of '55 Pontiac bumper ends.

Right - An old accessory straight bar was fitted into the cavity of Rick Snell's '50 Mercury and painted body color.

Below Left - This '51 Mercury sports a bold grille of vertical teeth that started out as bumper guards.

Below Right - 1950 Ford owner formed a molded opening to work around the canted quad headlights, then cut, bent and chromed bars of 1/2" tubing to fit the shape of the opening.

How To Build A Tube Grille

This 1960 Ford needed grilles for both front and rear. Copper tubing of 1/2 -inch diameter was chosen because copper takes chrome plating very well. Be careful not to select tubing of too large or too small diameter, since grille and cavity proportions are vital to the overall design.

The '60 Ford also has a large rear opening that lends itself to the grille treatment. Six bars were used for the front grille, while only four bars were used in back. Taillights fit behind the grille for a very effective custom appearance.

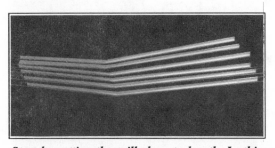

Start by cutting the grille bars to length. In this case the shape of the front and rear openings meant that virtually every tube was a different length. Front tubes were bent in the middle to conform to the shape of the grille opening and the contour of the hood. All this can be marked out in chalk on the floor to make sure everything is correct.

It is easiest to go ahead and take the time to make alignment jigs. Here the jig base is a simple piece of straight 1x6-inch lumber. Three pieces of sheetmetal were drilled with holes equidistant, and the lower edges bent over so the metal uprights can be clamped or bolted to the wood.

The tubing is placed through the end uprights and into the center locator, and checked to make sure every piece is aligned.

By Cris Boggess

In the good old days, there were aftermarket suppliers of tube grilles for most of the popular American cars. But now these grilles are hard to find. The solution is to make your own tube grille, which isn't too difficult for the competent backyard mechanic. One of the biggest problems is getting the grille plated after it is finished, but there are plating shops that will do small pieces without charging and arm and a leg. In this case, round tubing was used to build the grille, but square tubing can also be used. Solid stock can also be substituted, but the grille becomes quite heavy.

Bottom Left - The center jig upright is cut apart as shown in this sketch, so that only half the locating holes are slipped over the tubing. This is necessary to allow the upright to be removed after the tubing supports are installed.

Far Right - This sketch shows how the tubing is connected with braces that are brazed. Brass welding is necessary to mate the copper tubing to the sheet steel braces. Note that the outer braces are located on the inside off the jig uprights so that the jigs may be removed. Center brace is at the exact bend of the grille tubing.

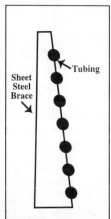
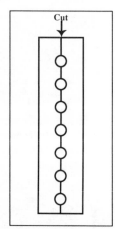

This tastefully customized '55 Ford 2-door hardtop makes use of a six-tube grille that bends rearward at the ends to hide the tube tips in the grille opening.

Six tubes fill the opening of this custom pickup. Note that the tips of each tube come to a point and three different tube lengths are used to create a grille that allows openings for the headlights.

Tube grilles are especially popular on custom trucks. This ten-tube grille fills the opening entirely, even covering

An example of a split grille, with five tubes up and two tubes down, all bent in the center, shows the kind of variety that can be accomplished when some thought is put into the problem of filling the grille opening with horizontal tubes.

Contoured around the headlights, this '64 Falcon makes use of seven tubes for its horizontal grille. Each tube is slightly different length, and all are rolled back at the ends.

Installing A '56 Chevy Grille

An example of how a stock grille from one car can be fitted to another is shown in this sequence of photos taken by Gene Winfield. In this case, a 1956 Chevy grille was being customized to fit into the grille opening of a 1949 Ford. But before the two could be mated, extensive custom work was done to the opening.

After stripping away all the stock grillework from the '49 Ford, the area around the grille opening was built up by welding in new sheetmetal pieces. A bit of hammer and dolly work straightened up the seams so that they would conform to the desired contour of the splash panel.

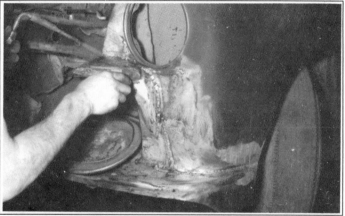

Lead sticks and a torch were used, along with a degree of skill, to cover the welded seams and to mold the panels into a smooth-flowing contour.

After all the grille opening modifications were made, the area was treated too a few moments with the grinder to smooth everything out.

To allow the grille to be bent at the center, to form a sharper angle, the '56 Chevy grille was disassembled and the horizontal bars were trimmed where they join the vertical support.

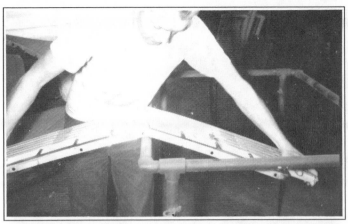

After reasembly, the center of the grille was bent over a pipe to get the desired angle for the nose.

New brackets needed to be made to attach the grille to the body. Measurements were taken and then a piece of 3/16" by 1" flat stock was bent to make the bracket.

Each of the four upper brackets was shaped different, ranging from roughly a "C" to an "L" to make the connection between grille and body. The lower part of the grille was simply bolted directly to the splash pan.

The finished product. Along with some other custom touches, the grille and grille opening look just right. The splash pan has been molded into the fenders, and the hood has been modified for a more aggressive appearance.

Bumpers

Left - The trim front bumper on Jack Walker's '50 Olds 88 is a '56 Olds bumper/grille top bar turned upside down.

Bottom Left - On the same car, builder Ray Goulart combined a '59 Chevy accessory bumper override bar with wrap-around tips from a '56 Buick to create the neat rear bumper over a rolled pan and molded gravel shield.

Bottom Right - '50 Dodge bumper was tucked in tight and welded to the body to form a strong molded pan.

By John Lee

Automobile bumpers are an enigma. On the one hand they are valuable as protection against body panel damage. On the other, they almost never seem to really be a part of the overall body design. Especially on American cars, where Detroit designers have had a penchant for changing bumper design from year to year, almost always going from good to bad to worse. Even so, over the years there have been some unique bumpers turned out by Detroit, and using a little creative genius, some of them can be adapted to a number of different cars. Most of the time, this will mean that new bumper brackets need to be made, but sometimes you can just reshape the existing brackets and drill new bumper mounting holes. The secret to bumper swapping is to take careful measurements of every bumper dimension height, width, depth, contours, brackets and plan carefully how to work this into the car's design.

If there is going to be radical front or rear customizing, this may be planned around the bumper shape. The customizer tries to integrate the bumper and body design, making a smooth transition from one to the other. Early on, the effort was to find a stock bumper that would do the job. Then, the more advanced builders started to modify bumpers, cutting and trimming and welding, and mixing parts. The chrome can be removed with a grinder, or the plating shop can use a reverse process to strip the chrome. Sometimes, the bumper is modified in shape and then welded to the body sheet metal. Of course, then the very purpose of a bumper is highly nullified.

Sectional bumpers offer the added advantage of being able to move the tips in or out to widen or narrow the bumper. If you want to do something different, you might consider merely turning a bumper upside down. This usually gives a lower appearance, and the splash apron can then be modified to fill any gaps.

If you want to smooth up the appearance of a bumper, the first thing to consider is filling the bumper bolt holes. Weld the bolt to the bumper directly behind the bolt hole, then fill the hole with weld (do not braze). Grind the weld to match the bumper contour, and finish the area with a very fine-grind sanding disc. The local plating shop will take care of the rest. Just remember that if you are going to have a plated bumper, rather than a painted unit, the bumper must really be smooth. Plating is not a filler like paint.

Right - For Larry Cochran's '50 Bel Air, Doug Thompson started with a one-piece California bar, molded in a '49 Chevy license guard and added '52 Pontiac overriders on the ends.

Left - John Eichinger's radical '40 Ford uses canted nerf bars that appear to be '50-'52 Pontiac override bars.

Right - The '57 DeSoto front bumper/grille has been a popular swap, shown here on John Kouw's '55 Buick. Main bar was left chrome while lower portion was painted for a rolled pan effect.

Below - Thin, nerf bar-type bumperettes protecting the rolled pan on this radical Chevy could appear to be hand-made.

Above - Clean split bumpers from '55 Pontiacs lend a custom touch. The wrap-around tips have been shortened and a frenched housing built to install them on this Mercury.

Left - 56 Chevy rear bumper has the right contours to work with the '56 Packard Clipper taillights. It would require a little narrowing to fit this '52-54 Ford.

Right - Nerf bars afford minimal protection while eliminating the standard bumper. These, bent in an S shape from round rod, are attached in the original bumper bracket position.

Below - A good-looking bumper-grille combination with lots of possibilities is the '56 Lincoln unit, installed here on a '56 Mercury.

Right - For his fat Buick convertible Jack Enos chose massive bumpers from a '46-48 Chrysler. Mounting bolt holes are filled, slim taillight lenses set in and old accessory exhaust tips attached to the bottom.

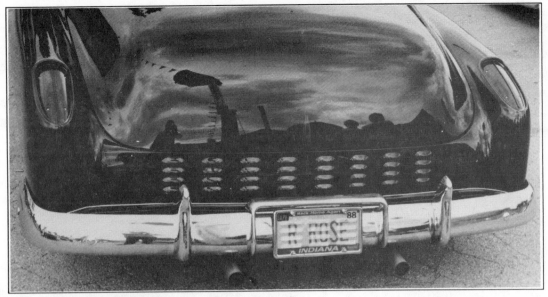

Right - 49 Chevy front license guards have always been popular, especially when the license is moved down to the bumper. They're hard to find, but Bumpers by Briz makes repros.

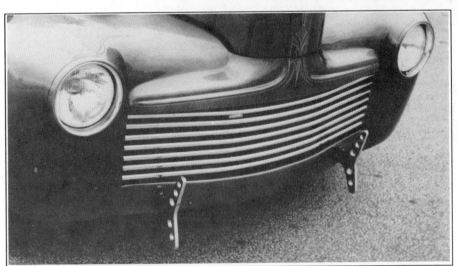

Left - Neat nerfs on this Ford have been cut from thick steel or aluminum plate, ground to shape, drilled with holes and polished or chromed.

Left - Another good-looking item that's hard to find is the license guard from a '52-53 Kaiser. End bombs have dimples that are natural for cutting out and running exhaust tips through.

Below - Clearing the deck and moving the license to the bumper, Gary Gerberding swapped a station wagon unit to his '55 Chevy Bel Air. It has an indentation for license mount and shorter guards.

ANTENNAS

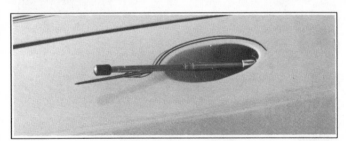

The antenna is very much a styling aspect of the custom car, whether it is traditional or modern, Today, however, most antennas are functional, while stub antenna were sometimes used just for effect on older customs (shades of dummy spotlights)!

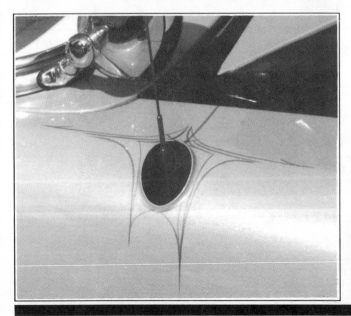

Frenched Antennas

Above - Bob Nordberg's '84 Chevy stepside pickup has the antenna in the front of the left rear fender.

Left - Twin antennas are tunneled into individual housings at the back of the right front fender of Bob Oman's '50 Mercury.

Right - Tunneled into the front of the slight fin on a '55 Pontiac rear quarter panel, radio aerial is fairly inconspicuous. Clean Poncho belongs to Jim Papouchis.

Far Right - Right rear quarter position was chosen by Ed Guffey for the single sunken antenna on his '50 Ford.

By John Lee

Radios are probably the most universally accepted accessories ever offered on automobiles. It's no longer a question of whether or not to have one, as it was 40 years ago. Today the decisions to be made are how powerful a unit to install, how many stereo speakers and whether to go for a graphic equalizer.

But great as they are, radios have always had one drawback: the antenna. The receiver won't pick up a thing without one, and it has to be sticking up or out from the body to pick up the signals.

Designers have tried various ways of integrating them into the styling and making them less obtrusive. Early Fords, Mercurys and Buicks had them on the roof above the center of the windshield, and some could even be turned down by an inside knob and "parked" on the center post when not needed. Cars of the

fifties made them part of the styling by mounting them on the rear fenders and deck lids with space ship-like bases and masts.

The best solution seems to be the power antenna, which can be retracted electrically when not in use. Some are even automatic, shooting up when the radio is turned on and telescoping back down when it's switched off. While some retract only to the level of the base, others disappear into a sunken housing.

Ironically, that's a trick custom builders have been using since the fifties, when the trend was to french the seams and integrate all the components of a car into a single unit.

Frenched antennas aren't hard to do, and they lend a finished, custom touch to a vehicle of any age or style. On the following pages we'll show you a couple different ways to carry out the job and give you an assortment of frenched antenna styles for early and late model customs and street rods.

The antenna base mounts below, and only the shaft comes through the rear deck of this '40 Chevrolet.

Dick Schultz tunneled the aerial into the front portion of the rear fender on his '51 Chevy.

Twin antennas on David Wolk's '50 Mercury are painted flat black and frenched into the front of the right door.

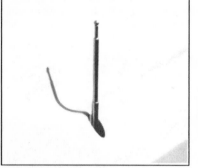

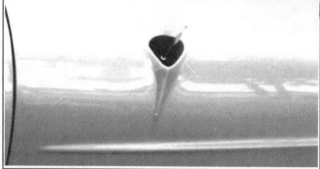

Terry Bross runs his aerial out of a tube frenched into the rear quarter of his '67 Chevelle station wagon that has the rear windows filled.

A triangular shaped hole was made for the antenna and molded into the fender of Denny Jackson's '53 Chevy with a fairing extending down on the fender.

Left and Above - The antenna on Harold Olsen's '48 Chevy retracts flush with the left front fender. Painted to match the body, the tip is barely visible.

Right and Below - Bill Mitchell balanced his '51 Chevy by installing one antenna on each front fender. Both are tunneled and frenched with a slight lip built up.

Above - 1950 Ford club coupe has its antenna projecting from a teardrop-shaped opening near the front of the rear quarter panel.

Above - According to Rick Squire, the power antenna tunneled into his '55 Chevy's fender cost $39.95 at the Western Auto store.

Left - A late-model GM product gave up its power antenna to Bob Bonnett's '57 Chevy. While not frenched, the compact unit retracts completely to be nearly flush with the fender.

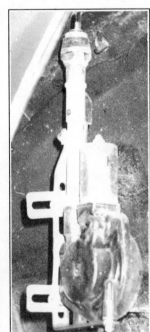

Above Left - A single mast is tunneled into a flush opening on John Povenmire's '66 Chevy Bel Air.

Above Right - Blue and burgundy pinstriping on the black body decorate the flaired opening on this '50 Mercury front fender.

Right and Above - The electric aerial on Mike McMillan's '40 Mercury is from the Gennie Shifter Company. It mounts beneath the fender with a combination of the brackets supplied and some Mike fabricated and welded to the cowl. The chrome tip is hardly noticed when down.

Simple Frenched Antenna

LaMont Woolen of Lincoln, Nebraska, was after the smooth look for his '49 Mercury coupe custom. Everything was to be frenched and molded in with no protrusions.

He and custom bodyman Rick Nantais determined that the least noticeable antenna installation would be a single power unit mounted in the trunk and protruding through a hole in the top of the right rear fender when extended. This required a hole of only an inch in diameter and flush with the body surface. The shaft is totally out of sight when retracted. The location is far enough behind the wheel well to allow plenty of room for mounting, and the outside hole is aligned with the top edge of the deck lid.

Rick could have mounted the antenna base inside the tube, but that would have required a tube at least 1 1/2 inches in diameter.

Instead, he used a one-inch tube and mounted the antenna base below it, with the shaft going through a rubber grommet (so it doesn't ground out against the metal).

Before welding it, he beveled the top end of the tube to follow the contour of the fender. To the bottom he welded a washer with a 3/8-inch hole in it for the grommet and shaft, and also a six-inch length of steel brake line tubing. A piece of rubber hose is slid onto the tubing and run out through a hole in the trunk floor to drain rain water out of the antenna hole.

Once the tube was made up, Rick welded it into the hole and finished it off on the outside. Then all that remained.was to weld in a bracket to mount the accessory antenna and wire it into the radio and the electrical system.

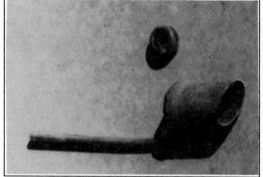

Make up the housing from a length of tubing. Insert it in the hole and hold it vertical to mark it for the curve of the body. Then cut and grind the top end to the correct contour.

Determine the desired location, which must have sufficient room below to mount the antenna. Then use a hole saw or drill and grinding stone to make a hole the size of the tube to house the antenna. Grind it out to a smooth, even edge.

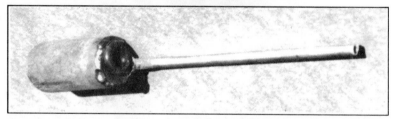

Weld a washer to the bottom of the tube. The rubber grommet goes into the washer hole to insulate the antenna shaft, which extends through it. Also drill a hole on one side of the bottom and weld in a length of brake line as a drain tube.

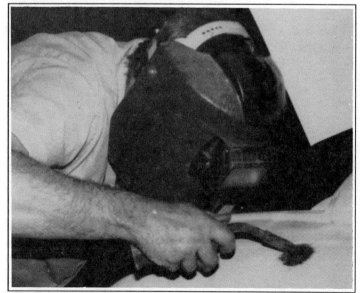

The closer the tube fits the hole, the less metal finishing you'll have to do. Tack weld the tube to the body. After checking alignment and position, weld the tube solidly into the hole.

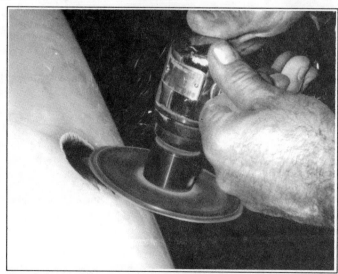

Grind the weld bead down even with the body surface and finish off smooth with a light coat of body filler if necessary to provide an even surface for priming and painting. Then fabricate a bracket inside the trunk for the antenna, mount it, hook up the wiring and run a rubber drain tube out the trunk floor.

Double Antenna Installation

by John Lee

The owner of this '60 Pontiac felt that dual antennas angled toward the rear fit the character of his car better than a single or vertical installation. Seeking a suitable housing, he noticed the oblong-shaped snorkle tube on the Pontiac's air cleaner. Cut off at an angle to fit the desired pitch of the antennas, it was welded into a matching hole cut between the taillight windsplits on top of the rear quarter panels.

The bottom of the tube housing was finished off in similar fashion to the installation previously described, with a sheet metal plate cut to shape, drilled for the two rubber grommets to hold the shafts and fitted with a small drain tube before being welded onto the tube.

In this case, the matching antennas were secured from a pair of mid-sixties Buicks in a junkyard. They are not powered, and only one is wired to the radio. Both are attached to the inner fender well by a length of steel strap. In finishing off the outside, a slight lip was built up around the opening to help keep some of the rain water out and to emphasize the teardrop shape.

A number of variations of this installation on different areas of the car are possible.

The snorkle tube on the '60 Pontiac air breather proved to be the desired size and shape for a dual antenna housing. It was cut off with a hack saw at the angle sought for the rearward pitch of the

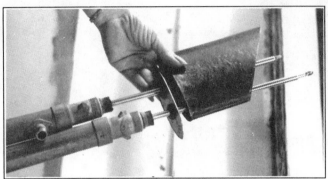

Exploded view shows the antenna shafts inserted through rubber grommets in a base cut from sheet stock to fit the bottom of the tube. The base must also be drilled at the lower corner and a drain tube welded in before welding to the tube.

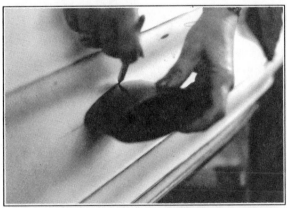

The tube centered between '60 Pontiac rear quarter windsplits served as a pattern to mark the hole to be cut out.

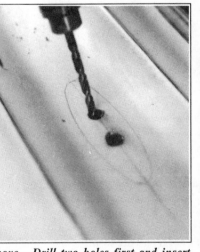

Above - Drill two holes first and insert the antennas to determine that positioning will be correct in relation to the mounting point inside the trunk. The hole can still be re-positioned at this point if necessary. If the position is right, go ahead and cut out the oval hole.

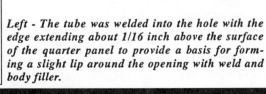

Left - The tube was welded into the hole with the edge extending about 1/16 inch above the surface of the quarter panel to provide a basis for forming a slight lip around the opening with weld and body filler.

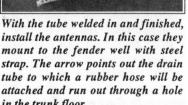

With the tube welded in and finished, install the antennas. In this case they mount to the fender well with steel strap. The arrow points out the drain tube to which a rubber hose will be attached and run out through a hole in the trunk floor.

Installing GM Electric Antennas

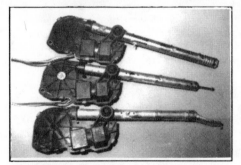

These Gm electric antennas are 17" in overall length.

These are the mast top with the various mount styles.

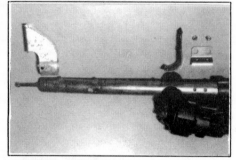

Inside the easily serviced motor.

by Dave McNurlen

Electric antennas are nice. Most regular fixed-mast antennas are hard to incorporate into an old car design without disturbing the body lines. You have the mast sticking there even when the car is shut off. With an electric, you can put the antenna in locations you might not put a fixed-mast type, because with the electric when it's not up it's not there.

From 1979 up, the GM cars that had electric antennas have used the same basic design. They've changed the way the mast tube mounts to the motor body and changed relay styles, but this is all just a refinement of the same '79 design. There were some electrics before '79, but they were kind of corn-ball compared to these new ones. The best of these having a black motor housing with a a handle-bar type mast mount. With these, only the mast is mounted solid to the car, and the motor has a little shock-absorber action from the doughnut mount grommets. The '79 style masts mounted directly to the motor seemed to be noisier, and broke mast-drive cables more than the later design.

There are three basic mast types. Threaded bezel mount, welded bracket mount, and universal. The threaded bezel screws into the top of the mast. The bracket mount is designed for specific cars, and the universal is what you get from the dealer parts department.

With the threaded mount, all of the bezels will interchange, as GM only used one thread size. You can pick the style you want and there's usually an extra inch of bezel thread, to allow the black grommet that compensates for differences in angle between the body and the bezel.

The mast that has brackets welded to it can either be used as-is or the spot-welded brackets can be removed by drilling out the welds. It's only necessary to drill through the bracket (3/8" maximum), since going too far into the mast tube itself could damage the antenna.

The mast with bracket in the pictures is from an '86 Cutlass Ciera. It uses a two-piece bezel that attaches to the fender. The mast comes out of the fender side at an angle equal to the non-parallel part of the bracket.

The universal mast is exactly that. It's designed to be used on a maximum number of GM cars as a parts replacement for broken antennas. It has mount holes 360 degrees around at top and bottom so various brackets can put it in almost anything. The bracket attaching screws are only 1/4" long, as anything longer might ground the mast out or damage it.

All of these masts have an end tip that screws n, leaving open the possibility of custom-designed ends.

The antenna is connected to the radio by a coaxial cable. It attaches to the mast either directly, or with a screw-on connector,

at a post near the bottom of the mast. 1985 Buick Electras used a trunk-mount antenna, so that coax will be one of the longest. Some of these coax cables are kind of strange, with several different types of connectors, so just make sure you've got a connector system that will all hook up.

To make all this stuff work, the antenna has to go up and down. GM had several antenna and relay combinations, and some wires are switched from year to year, and car to car so it's a good idea to get the antenna and relay from the same car. Be sure to get the relay connectors at that time too, as they are very hard to find elsewhere. The wire colors have remained consistent through the years and that will help in locating the relay. You'll probably find it either behind or under the glove-box area.

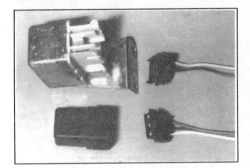
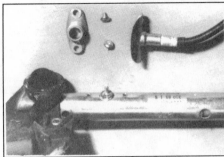

Far Left - The two antennas coax designs; note how short the mount screws are.

Left - The two relay designs and the connectors from the antenna.

Breaker 1 - 9

Lots of rodders like to use a CB. In the early and mid-eighties, GM sold alot of combination AM-FM-CB radios. Quite a few Cadillacs, Oldsmobiles, and Buicks had them. They used this same electric antenna design with a "load-coil" on the mast, and a "signal splitter" in the coax to separate the AM-FM and CB signals. The splitter is usually behind the glove-box in most GM cars and has the three coax leads hooked to it. The CB mast and splitter have to be used as a combination to work properly. There was sometimes a short stub lead taped to the side of the mast tube, coming out of an extra coax connector, but that seems to depend on model.

If you want the antenna up with the car turned off, put a toggle switch in the 12 volt power circuit to shut off power to the relay once the mast is up.

Tidbits

Testing the motor:
- Green-12 Volts, Gray-ground/UP
- White-12 volts, Green-ground/DOWN

Part numbers and prices over the GM counter (prices approximate):
- '84 Olds 88 relay 22510577, $16.00
- '79 Olds 88 relay - 556511, $13.00
- 84 Olds 88 mast and tube - no CB - 22048584, $64.00
- 84 Olds 88 mast and tube - w/CB - 22048583 $64.00
  (Both of the above use a threaded bezel mount)
- CB splitter - 25512518, $58.00
- 84 Olds 88 elec. antenna assembly - 22048604, $94.00

Thanks to Woody and Richard at Meador Olds Parts Department, Fort Worth, Texas, for the numbers. Some GM '88s and most '89s use a totally new antenna design, but still use the same black relay

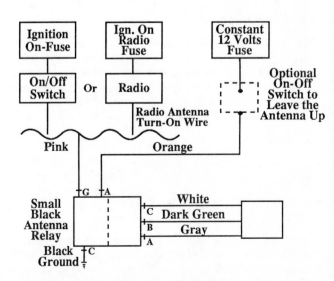

UPHOLSTERY

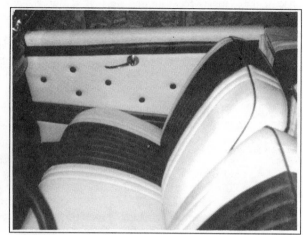

I t's amazing the things that have found their way into service as automotive upholstery. Everything including sheepskin rugs, silkscreened t-shirts and grandma's knit doily has been draped across a seat either to improve comfort, to make a statement or just to cover a hole.

But when it comes to custom upholstery of a higher order, Denny Nish has spent upwards of three decades building a reputation for some of the finest work around. He is an expert when it comes to quality materials and craftsmanship, so we asked him to fill us in on the finer points of custom upholstery.

There are two aspects to an upholstery job -- labor and materials. Quality in either area costs money. You may select the finest materials and then try to cut costs in the labor column only to be dissatisfied with the result. Likewise, if you buy expert labor but try to cut costs in the materials, the result may be less than you had hoped for. Upholstery work is one thing that shouldn't be budgeted too tight, because it is highly visible and is one of the features of a custom car that is most appreciated by onlookers.

At a good shop, the labor cost is the same regardless of the quality of material being used, so if you're already paying for good craftsmanship, you might as well get the best material available. Invariably, the better materials are more durable and maintain their fine appearance longer than cheaper stuff.

Materials

Materials fall into three basic categories: leather, vinyl, and fabric. According to Nish, approximately 85% of his upholstery work is now being done in leather. There is no other material that can rival properly cared-for, high quality top-grain leather for durability. Some of the best upholstery leather comes from Scotland and is vat dyed in England or Italy.

Next down the durability list from leather is vinyl. But as with everything else, there is high-quality and low-quality vinyl. For an expensive custom car, you want the best you can get, and that's going to cost between $20 and $25 per yard for first-quali-

ty vinyl. Domestic vinyl material of first-quality is available in names like Naugahyde (Uniroyal), or Voltaflex (General Tire). German vinyl is also a favorite in fine upholstery shops.

Fabric materials (velours and tweeds) are quite popular, and again, some are good and some are not so good. U.S. government regulations have resulted in a decreased quality of domestic fabrics. Colors fade more easily than they used to because the dye process has been changed. Today, German and Italian fabrics are the best, unless you go to aircraft-quality fabric, which costs in the neighborhood of $50 to $70 per yard.

Stitching is done mostly for cosmetic or decorative reasons. Some stitch patterns are quite traditional, such as tuck 'n roll, diamond tuck, etc., but others fall into the "high-tech" category where design creativity can really show off. Regardless of what stitch pattern is employed, dacron thread is the right thread to use. Hardly anybody uses cotton thread anymore, but when you're having your interior work done you don't want to take any chances, so specify dacron thread.

Some upholstery jobs call for the use of glue to hold things together. High/low panels are put together this way, and they are generally quite durable.

Polyfoam padding material is commonly used in most upholstery applications today. Again, quality ranges from high to low. Generally, the heavier the density, the better the quality -- but only up to a point. Sometimes, manufacturers start adding too much filler to increase the density of the foam, but that doesn't add to the quality. Aircraft-quality foam padding is good stuff.

When stiffeners are are needed for upholstered panels, such as for door panels, there is a choice to make. The selection ranges from aluminum to fiberglass to waterproof panel board. Nish works exclusively with aluminum panels, which he says are easier and faster to work with than fiberglass. He cautions that in a humid environment, waterproof panel board proves itself to be less than totally impervious to the effects of moisture. It can swell and warp.

If you deal with a local upholstery shop that does fine work, but cannot get some of the materials we have talked about, get ahold of Nish Interiors, 3585 West Twain, Bldg. C, Las Vegas, Nevada 89103; (702) 362-7610. Denny can serve as your supply source.

Selecting A Shop

It was once popular to head south, across the border, for a quick and dirty upholstery job. Back in the '50s and '60s, Tijuana was a Mecca for teenagers enrolled in the religion of cheap tuck 'n roll. And, apparently, that still exists today. As might be expected, a word of caution is issued here. When it comes to open heart surgery or upholstery work, be careful. Although the price might be appealing, you want your custom to last a long time and stand up to the daily use of a driven vehicle. Real customs are driven, you know. Materials used as automotive upholstery padding in Tijuana shops can range from shredded paper to cotton to low-quality foam.

Even stateside, selecting a shop to do the work is a matter of common sense. If someone tells you they will upholster a seat for $100, using the highest quality vinyl, and you know it involves the use of 3 yards of material that costs $20 to $25 per yard, hang onto your wallet. These guys may be stuffing your seat with diapers and covering them with trash bags.

As with all other aspects of the custom car hobby, shopping for a service such as upholstery work calls for a little sniffing around. Ask the shop manager for some referrals from past customers, then go talk with these customers about their satisfaction with the work performed. Ask to see some examples of their more difficult work. Find out if their shop has ever been involved in working on a show car, and if so find out if the car has won any awards especially for upholstery. Talk materials, and see if they mention any of the right names.

Custom Alternative

There are other ways of coming up with a custom interior besides going to a custom upholstery shop. You may decide to swap the seats of one car into another. Some stock seats are especially popular for this, such as the wrap-around rear seats of a mid-sixties Thunderbird, or the big, plush, pillow-back seats of modern luxury cars. This kind of seat swapping can result in more than just a custom interior appearance. You may also wind up with power seats, recliners, fold-down arm rests, and other functional features.

Care And Maintenance

When it comes to care and maintenance of a custom interior, there are a few Do's and Don'ts

1. Leather should be oiled about once a month in order to keep it soft and supple.
2. Although it is a common practice to apply a vinyl treatment to vinyl material, Nish cautions against it, saying that it makes the vinyl hold heat, prevents it from breathing and gives the material an artificial coating.
3. Cleaners with ammonia should be avoided because they dry out vinyl.
4. Solvent-type cleaners shouldn't be applied to vinyl upholstery material on a day-to-day basis, but reserved for those infrequent heavy cleaning jobs.
5. Under no circumstances apply a lacquer thinner to a vinyl surface because it will destroy it.

The best advice for prolonging the life of vinyl material and keeping it looking good is to simply keep it clean. Ordinary dishwashing soap and water will do the job most of the time. For fabric materials, commercially available velour and carpet cleaners work well. For best results, be sure to follow the directions on the product package.

Traditional upholstery of the classic era is tuck 'n roll. In the case of this custom, the upholstery theme was carried through to the trunk and engine compartment as well.

High-tech stitch patterns give the upholsterer a chance to create unique styling for the custom interior.

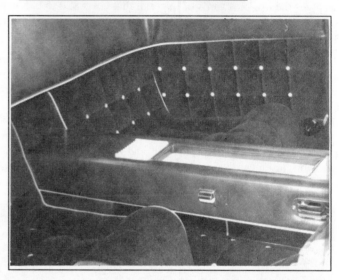

Button tuft is a traditional upholstery style that brings back memories of the early days of customizing. Here, the entire interior is custom built and the upholstery work displayed on the steering wheel cover and in the trunk.

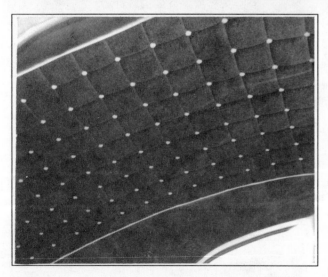

Modern luxury seats are finding their way into the interiors of early customs. This not only increases the comfort level but lends a high-tech appearance. Consider the plush pillow-back seats and full recliners for the ultimate in cruisin' comfort. Some of these front buckets feature electric operation. Unique stitch patterns can be created on door panels and carried over to the rear seat interior side panels, if desired. With a little work, a classic rear seat and all the surrounding sheetmetal like the wrap-around mid-sixties Thunderbird can be made to work in a custom.

PAINT

To emphasize the straight, horizontal lines of the '75 Thunderbird, David McNary applied bands progressing from light gray to dark gray to black along the lower panels. The main color is white. Graphic designs of the same shades were applied to the hood and deck lid.

by John Lee

Color. You might say it's the major impact of your car. The proof of the pudding. The crowning glory.

To begin with, the color or finish is the first impression the viewer's eye sends to the brain. It can affect the amount of time he or she concentrates on the car -- or your car.

A bright color or multiple colors blending and contrasting can convey the message, "This car is hot!" or "This car is something special!" It invites the bystander to take a close look.

Wild graphics and flames send out a similar message, suggesting a machine with zip and power. A thorough inspection of the engine compartment and drive train is suggested.

Custom painters and bodymen know it's the dark colors that magnify any flaws in the metal bending and filling they've done to the car's body. Thus, black or dark, solid purples, burgundys, browns and blues draw the spectator's eye to examine the quality of the work.

Pinstriping can add another dimension to the finish, replacing a bit of decoration where other forms of decoration have been removed. Pinstriping also draws attention to unique styling features that have been incorporated.

Finally, exhibiting a finely-executed paint job is a signal that the vehicle is a finished project. The design, an expression of the owner's and/or builder's tastes, has been satisfactorally executed.

As anyone who's been to a car show or race meet in the last couple years is well aware, there are no hard and fast rules governing the application of color and design to custom-built motor vehicles. Flames, stripes, graphics, solids, stripes, "hot" and "cool" colors -- one can see them all at whatever automotive gathering he chooses to attend.

On the following pages are a few of the "major impact" statements we've run across recently. Look 'em over. Maybe one or a combination is just what you've been needing to individualize your chariot!

Above - Stephanie Reinke's '77 Trans Am is burgundy with a single pink neon graphic stripe running down each side and pink pinstripe designs highlighting various features.

Right - 1984 Thunderbird of Larry James is white with blackout trim. Larry has added a pair of graphic stripes in red and burgundy which trail back along the sides and across the deck lid.

Below - The finish is dark blue, flames light blue and pinstriping pink and blue on Doug and Diane Fry's '78 Datsun mini truck. License is set into striped air dam,

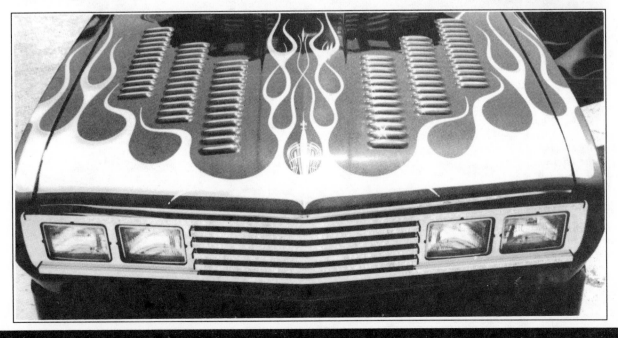

While '55 Pontiac side trim separates light and dark purple two-toning on Joe Koenigsmark's '50 Mercury, thin silver scallops outline the rounded hood corners and frenched headlights and trail back from the wheel housings.

Rather than try to adapt chrome for the trim effect he wanted, M. Balke had Buick-style sweepspears painted on his '47 Chevy coupe by airbrush. Shading and highlighting make it look like chrome from a few steps away.

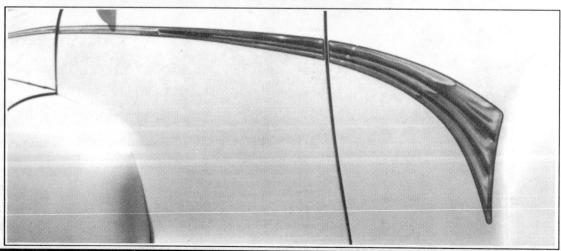

Above - The pinstriper putting flames on R. Winkler's '37 Ford didn't even stop at the window! The coupe is purple, flames red and white.

Right - The same coupe pays tribute to Marilyn Monroe with a depiction on the decklid of her famous scene from "Some Like It Hot."

Flames are gold and red and the main finish is black on Dan Marshall's chopped '55 Chevy sedan delivery. Notice flames on the roof and the "Iron Mistress" name in gold leaf on the panel sides.

Asymmetric graphic designs like this were popular during the 1960s. In fact, Dick Brandt's '58 Corvette could have been done then. Gold and purple are combined in the graphic over a yellow body.

Above - A cove outlined by stainless trim as on this '58 Pontiac Star Chief is a natural to contain a flame design. Here the fiery fingers are metallic turquoise against a black background.

Right - Sharp reflections testify to the quality of the bodywork and the '79 Lincoln Midnight Blue lacquer on J.T. Winfrey's '37 Ford Cabriolet. To set off the monochromatic paint job, Roger Ward masked off a strip and a set of squiggles at the beltline and painted on a light blue stripe, bordered with thin pinstripes.

A spider web complete with spider is painted on the right front fender of thie '47 Olds convertible to set off the tunneled radio antenna.

The '55 Ford Mainline came with no bright side trim, leaving it ripe for a custom paint treatment like this tapered stripe extending down the side and wrapping over the deck lid. The stripe is blue on a white body with pinstriping in blue and pink.

Ribbons of flame emanate from the grille and headlight areas of this '40 Ford and trail back across hood and doors.

Black '49 Plymouth is unaltered except for top chop and lowering. Flames change color from white through yellow to orange and red over a black base.

Above - Chopped Chevy pickup is painted white with panels, flames and stripes in shades of blue.

Below - Black shoebox Ford comes alive with an elaborate scheme of scallops and pinstripes in light blue.

Building A Show Winner

Tricks of the trade that make the difference between a champion and an also ran!

It is a whole different world, that of show cars and trucks. The chrome is the same (almost), as is the glittering paint (almost), and the vibrant upholstery (almost). Within that different world, to be a champion may mean something as incidental as paint overspray on a hidden frame member or a spot of grease on a tie rod end.

In the restoration hobby, it is generally said that a 100 point vehicle represents the ultimate perfection, a machine that is far superior to what it was when new. And, the difference between a 95 point car and a 100 point car can equal thousands and thousands of dollars.

For the hot rod and custom car enthusiast, the ultimate vehicle is not so much a matter of money as it is of labor, assuming that the enthusiast can do the majority of his own work. But, whether the builder does his own work, or farms it out, there are some very specific tricks (and common sense) of the show trade.

The first step in building a show winner is to determine exactly how serious the vehicle will be in show competition. The assumption is that the vehicle is already constructed, or very nearly so. If show competition is to be very serious, it is wise to visit several area shows and carefully inspect similar vehicles. Talk to the vehicle owners, as well as show producers and judges. Every region of the nation will have peculiarities...types of cars that are most popular, items that the judges consider more important, show building limitations, numbers of spectators, etc. Learn these things before showing the vehicle, if possible.

If the vehicle is to be shown only casually, then chances are it will probably not win the overall top prizes. Even in the street driven classes, where the vehicle is assumed to be driven many miles a year, the vehicle that is best prepared for the show will win. Attention to detail is the first order of show preparation, once the decision is made to be competitive in show judging.

If the vehicle will only be shown locally, there may or may not be an advantage in belonging to the International Show Car Association (ISCA). However, if the vehicle is to be shown in several area shows, there is a definite advantage to being an ISCA member. Many ISCA shows pay tow money, as do some non-ISCA shows. This is usually so much per mile, one way. At ISCA shows there is also the possibility that awards will include cash prizes, so that a successful show vehicle may break even, or make a slight profit, because of the show. For full information on ISCA, write to 32365 Mally Drive, Madison Heights, MI 48071.

When building a car that will be shown competitively, it is a matter of going the "extra mile" in preparing the overall car. Keep in mind that the show judges will consider giving show points to the vehicle as they inspect five basic categories: Body, interior, undercarriage, engine, and safety. The object is to garner the maximum number of allowable points in these areas, and to do this the builder must pay maximum attention to detail in each area. As the judge looks at each area, he will keep two things uppermost in mind...degree of difficulty (of making the change or restoration), and quality of execution. It is in the little things where points begin to pile up, and it is here where the tie-breakers are determined.

What appears to be a dynamite vehicle might be nothing more than a good exterior paint job. Closer inspection might reveal a lack of detailing, and such a vehicle is quickly out of contention for the big prizes. Judges will very carefully look at the finish on door jambs, under the fender wells, nooks and crannies in the engine compartment... just about every hidden area possible.

When painting the vehicle, take the extra time to prepare all the "raw edges". Remove the doors so that every parting of the door jambs can be filled and sanded smooth. Remove the hood, and fill/sand around everything, even the areas that can't be seen readily. Smooth the edges of the fender opening, finish inside the grille cavity, don't leave any area undone. During painting, take the extra time to make sure that each of these areas gets excellent treatment. Just a small spot of overspray, or unpainted surface, and the award can go elsewhere.

This attention to detail extends to the upholstery. Do not leave any frayed edge showing, clean everything until it is near spotless. Make all the trim fit exactly.

When working with vehicle accessories, whether in the engine compartment, passenger area, or on the exterior, make sure the accessories are harmonious. Don't add something just for the sake of addition. For example, if braided stainless plumbing is used in the engine compartment, it probably should be used for everything. This keeps the theme constant. At the same time, try to keep everything uncluttered. Don't overdo, and don't underdo. Keep in mind that it is very possible to create beyond the experience of the judges (although this is highly unlikely at the better shows). For instance, a super high tech machine may be so understated that the judges fail to see that the degree of difficulty in making something "trick" far exceeds the norm.

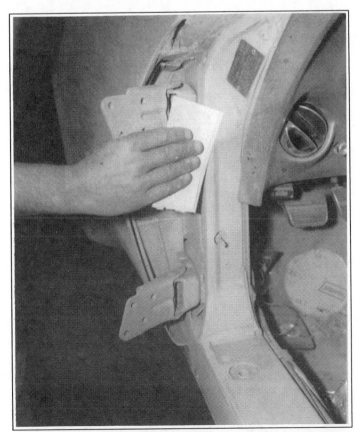

Much of show preparation begins with an outstanding paint job, and excellent paint means removal of doors, hood, deck lid, etc. After door is removed, finish jambs as well as outside of body.

Paying attention to detail extends even to the nuts and bolts. In an area where there is a line of screw heads, take the time to "slot" or "index" the screw head slots. That is, make them all line up. It is a little thing, but doing it pays dividends.

Also pay strict attention to the vehicle class rules. This is another excellent reason for joining ISCA and using their rule book as a building guide. If your particular class is allowed a set number of modifications, then if you do even a small modification extra, you can be in another classification. This might be something as innocent as filling a body seam with sealer. Incidentally, seams should always receive attention. After the body has been prepared for paint, but before paint is added, always clean out the seams and recaulk. One trick of the trade is to caulk a seam, then run a knife blade or hacksaw blade down the seam. This smooths the area, and still makes it look like it is factory original. While paying attention to class rules, it is generally necessarily to build to the maximum of the rules if the vehicle is to be a serious competitor. If 5 modifications are allowed, it may be that all five are necessary to win. The biggest temptation to overcome is the tendency to overbuild.

Rule of thumb for all serious show builders is that the better the car (and the more well known it becomes), the more it will be picked apart by the judges. The better you are at preparing a show car, the more that is expected!

The ISCA rulebook contains a special section on how to show a vehicle for championship points. In the show circuit, there is a championship competition, a competition that can sometimes reach heroic proportions. Even so, the first timer can (and often does) beat the seasoned expert, especially if he has a good vehicle and has followed the ISCA advice.

For instance, always point out to the judges any unusual, be noted, so the judge can look at them, and the car should be so displayed that the judges can look everywhere. Before and during show hours! Remember this, because some judging is done when there are no spectators present, and many a first place trophy has passed along because the exhibitor "closed shop" when the building doors were shut.

Always show the best side of the vehicle to the public, but don't try to hide any mistakes or imperfections. The judges are experienced enough to pick up on this right away. The judges give points only for what they can see, but they will deduct points for what they discover, as well. Clean the vehicle thoroughly, including the undercarriage (exception to this would be the special Street classes, where the undercarriage is often not judged for cleanliness).

A good display is always recommended, and here the secret is to be good but not gaudy. The display draws attention to the vehicle, and can even be utilized to emphasize the vehicle strong points. Example: Fully chromed undercarriage, so mirrors are essential. Do not build a display that overpowers the vehicle, and do not create a display that is too large for the building(s). When there might be concern about a display, always contact the show promoter well in advance.

Also, always enter a show as much in advance as possible. Some shows pay tow money only to the first so many exhibitors, and in some cases, the first-come-best-display-spot-in-the- building applies.

Ultimately, the best advice for getting involved with building a winning show car is to enter the shows and learn the ropes. You may win the first time out, and you may not, but you will certainly know far more at the end of the show than when it began. Just beware of one thing...car shows can be habit forming!

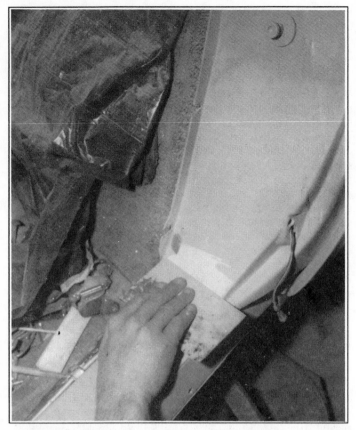

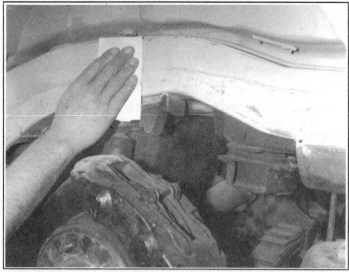

Above Left - Pay particular attention to the imperfections that are bound to be apparent on door jambs, use filler sparingly and finish very smooth.

Above Right - A little thing often overlooked is recaulking of all factory caulked body seams. Do not caulk seams that were not filled originally, paint over the compound.

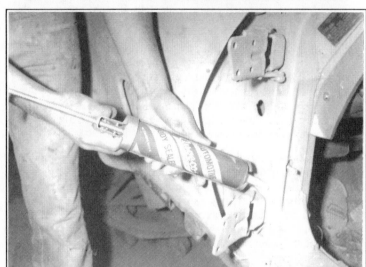

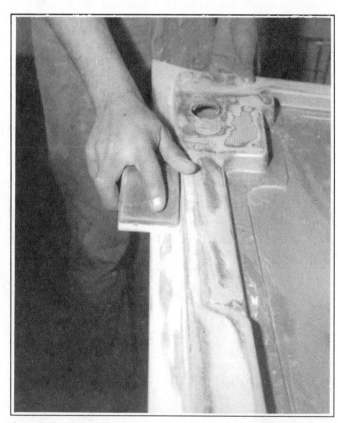

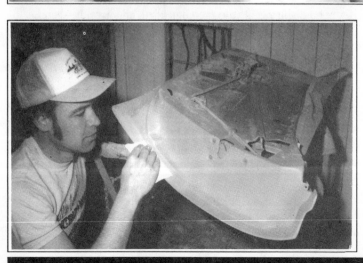

Above Left - Even the frame needs attention, as will the suspension parts.

Above Right - Edges of all opening panels should be very carefully sanded, filled, and sanded again. This is particularly true of the hood inside edges, which are readily seen by judges.

Left - Inner edges of doors need the filling and sanding routine, total amount of time doing this is negligible considering how many extra points this attention is worth.

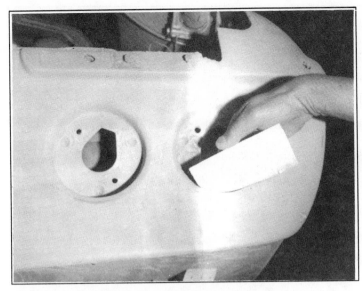

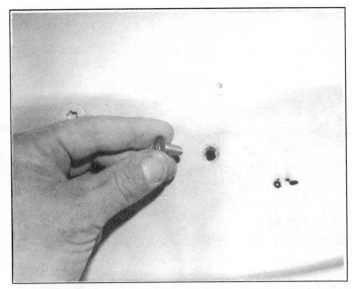

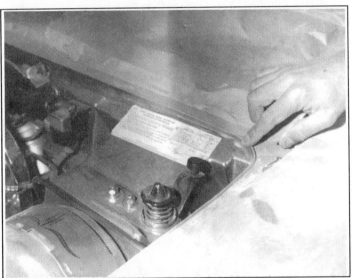

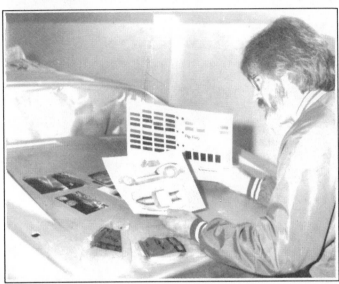

Top Left - And don't overlook areas that seem to be inconsequential, such as upper overhang of recessed lights. Judges will feel in these areas to determine quality of work.

Top Right- Here special recessed head screws replace the more common factory items, a little plus that adds to detail.

Above Left - The little nooks and crannies in the engine compartment opening should be finished as well as any place on the car.

Above Right- Vette owner John Moore looks over color charts and design drawings for graphics on his show winner. Selection of color scheme is extremely important when going after the biggest prize.

Left - Custom paint whiz Carl Brunson color sands the Corvette body. This foundation must be flawless, new acrylic paints provide superior finishes.

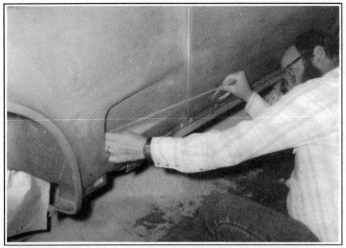

After final clear coat is dried on the car, pin stripper and graphics designer Brooke Passey starts the arduous task of taping off the design. Note how side spears emerge from front fender scoop.

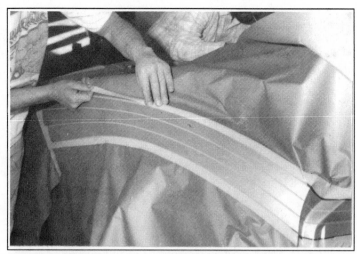

Brunson and Passey tape perimeter of graphics with paper, a good taping job determines how well the finish graphics will appear.

This is where attention to detail begins to show. Side graphics are carried over to the door jamb.

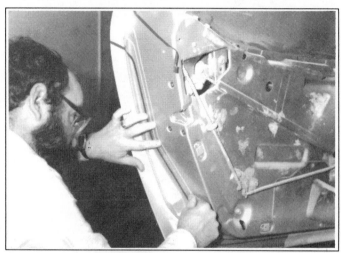

Use the narrow masking tape especially made for making very tight bends, as Passey does on door facing. By carrying graphics through door opening, extra detail catches judges eye.

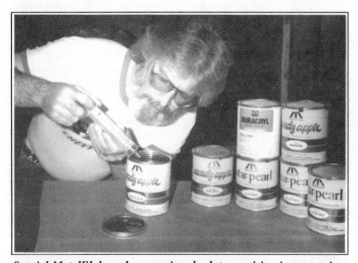

Special MetalFlake colors require absolute precision in measuring, John Moore found an animal syringe from agriculture supplies store ideal for the purpose.

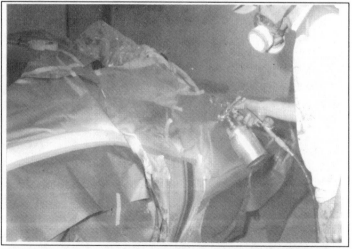

With tape in place, Brunson starts the hours-long task of applying special colors. Be very patient at this stage, since final results are made here.

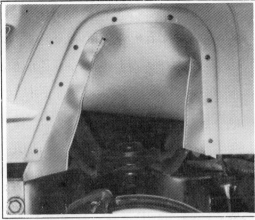

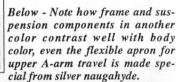

Below - Note how frame and suspension components in another color contrast well with body color, even the flexible apron for upper A-arm travel is made special from silver naugahyde.

Above Left - Once the graphics are applied, tape/paper are removed and edges of the graphics are color sanded. In this case, finger tips cannot tell where paint lap is. Passey chose to apply highlight striping to center of each spear, which serves to emphasize quality of the paint work.

Above Center - Since wheels are removed for show display, inner fender panels are also finished perfectly, then striping is added for highlights.

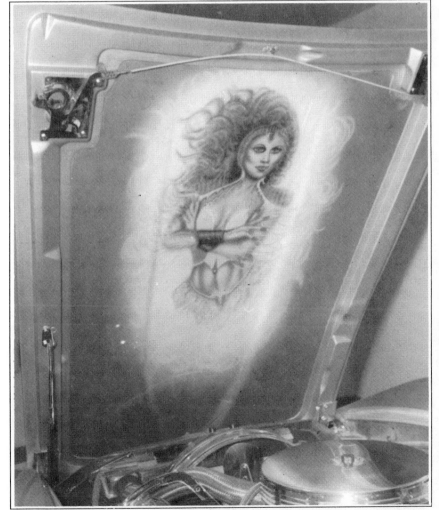

Passey utilized talents as an artist to create mural on underside of hood, the extra colors serve to enhance the chromed engine impact.

After graphics are applied to door facing, weatherstripping is very carefully glued in place. The effect is one of maximum attention to the paint scheme.

EXAMPLES

Turning A Sedan Into A Convert—

In December 1951, Grandpa bought a new 1951 Buick 4-door sedan for Grandmother…as a Christmas gift. Years later, when she was no longer able to drive, due to poor vision, Grandma passed the car along to Ray Bozarth. When he pulled it home the motor was frozen (with only 28,000 miles!), but otherwise it was in fine condition.

It stayed in a storage building for years, while Ray and Myrna tried to decide what to do with it. In 1986, the pair had M.K. John of Muscatine, Iowa draw up a design of the car as it might appear customized. The result was a 2-door, Carson topped, nosed and decked beauty. But…the car was a 4-door. M.K. figured that Merlin Berg of Bellevue, Iowa could change that little incidental factory oversight.

So, off to Bellevue, where Merlin said, "Yes, I can do it." And do it he did. From Merlin's shop it went to Jim McFall for the interior. All three of these men are outstanding creative talents, as is obvious. At the Kustom Kemp Nationals in Holland, Michigan this summer, Grandma's Christmas present turned out to be a Plum Wild hit with everyone.

The Buick with stock straight eight engine and original front suspension. There is a tremendous amount of room in the engine compartment to accept just about any kind of power selected.

Below - A frame clip from a late model GM makes an excellent substitute for the Buick, centerline of the new clip wheels is placed in same place as Buick, lots of gusset material is used to ensure maximum strength at graft point.

 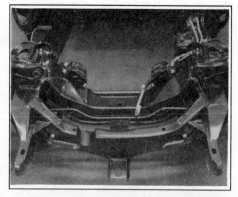 

Many modifications were made to the Buick chassis, notch in front secondary crossmember is for radiator hose. Original trans crossmember has extended pad for Turbo automatic, X-member has been cut away and rebuilt for higher level of driveshaft (due to lowering of car at rear). Note how upper area of rear spring perch now has towers, so rear of car is this much lower, large bolts allow adjustment of spring height. While building it is necessary to guesstimate chassis ride height, here bags of cement were piled on crossmember to simulate body weight.

With powertrain in place it is possible to run the entire exhaust system before replacing the body. With the driveline running higher in the body it is often necessary to fabricate a new driveshaft tunnel, in this case the entire floor area over rearend and a portion of flooring midbody was replaced with new sheetmetal.

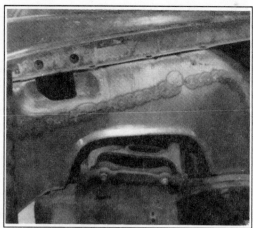

Body can be lifted from chassis with hoist or with jack-stands, in such a project the body is up and down often for fitting. When making any chassis changes it is vital to get the wheels in exact location of fender openings, sometimes when front end is lowered the front wheels tend to move backward in opening, this must be compensated for during construction. When a frame clip is added, inner splash panels usually need reworking. After all the frame work was done on Buick, the frame was stripped, sandblasted, and painted.

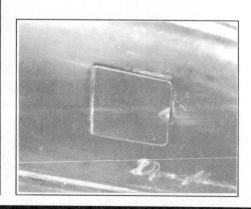

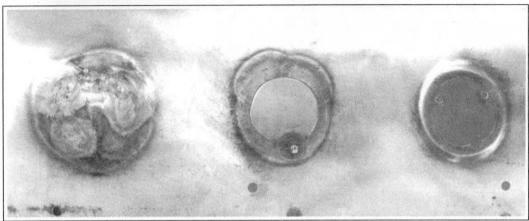

Although chassis/powertrain work on the Buick is extensive, the bodywork is more so. Gas filler cap was removed by welding in a flush piece of metal, as were the famed Buick portholes in front fenders. At the rear, stock taillights were removed and new lights installed, masking tape was used to get a general idea of how new lights would look.

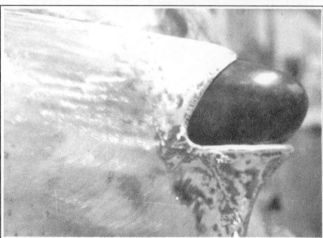

Top corner of rear fender was cut away, new taillight lens set in place and metal base fabricated. Small bar stock or tubing can be bent to fit lens tightly and give the final frenched look. Side trim was positioned across both doors to determine how much stock front door had to be lengthened to duplicate original two-door.

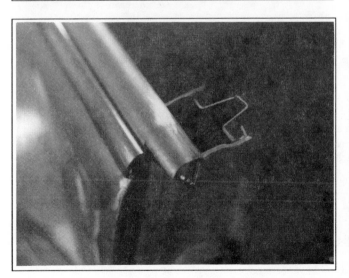

Entire door post was removed from floorpan and just above window opening, rear door panel was trimmed to new size (note side trim spear in place as a guide), then door post was repositioned aft of four-door location. Trimmed rear door skin is tack welded in position on quarter and relocated door post, roll at top of door is extended slightly so that door fits better. Piece cut from front of rear door is then welded to back of front door.

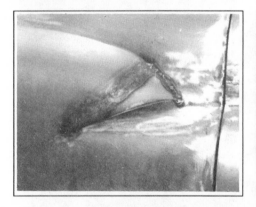

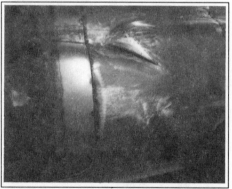

Builder Merle Berg reshapes the top of the sedan door, only a stub of the front window guide was retained to give the door glass stability. Before the rear door skins were shortened, Berge reshaped the metal to create a slanted scoop effect, again using tubing/bar stock so the opening edge would be rounded. The entire rear skirt area was created to flow into the shape of the Buick side trim. Nearly everything done to this car has been covered in the first part of this book.

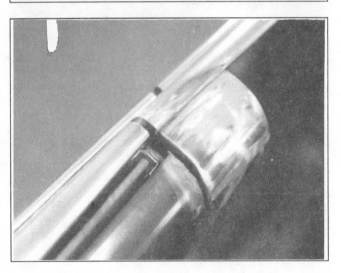

The sequence of adding the longer door panel and making everything fit would apply to virtually any four door being turned into a two door hardtop or convert. Note in the last photo of this sequence how the top of the door post has been rounded off and top of front door actually insets slightly so that door glass and portion of inner side of door does not have to be extended same as door skin.

When the top panel is trimmed away from the windshield area, inner support is exposed. This metal was trimmed and bent horizontal so that convert top would mate, curved edges of windshield frame were straightened at upper corners. This is the area where many sedans- turned-convertibles do not receive enough work and the result is a vehicle that looks exactly like a cut-up closed car. Most converts have a rather square look to the windshield top and sides, the filler used on the windshield posts can be plastic if it is thin. If it is going to be thick then lead should be used.

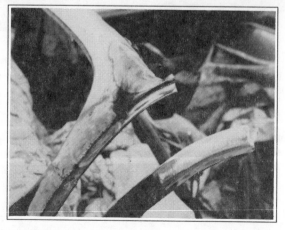

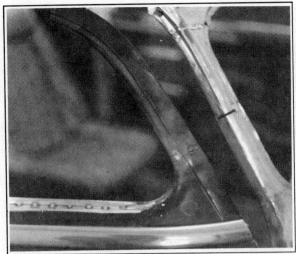

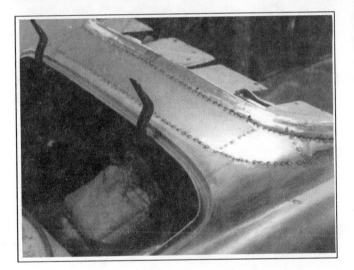

Because the convertible top is shorter than the sedan, the Buick panel between deck lid and top was lengthened. Original package tray and window support structure was cut and moved forward, then pieces of sheetmetal added to fill the gap. Here, as with most other places where thin sheetmetal was used, a MIG welder was selected and all initial work was done with tack welds. This will keep distortion to a minimum on all flat as well as curved areas. Usually all that is needed is to grind excess weld metal off and add only a thin layer of plastic filler to get excellent finish.

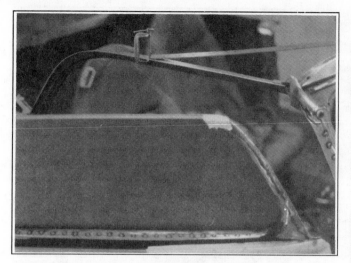

Board templates of the door glass were made up, then the top structure was started by using bar stock and channel bent over the glass area. If a collapsible convertible top were to be used, some late model top mechanism would have been modified to fit and the door glass/quarter glass made to fit. In this case, the padded top needs a support structure because the original top skin was trimmed away flatter to fit the support. Using a fiberglass or metal sub-skin is becoming a very popular way to achieve a relatively lightweight padded Carson-style top.

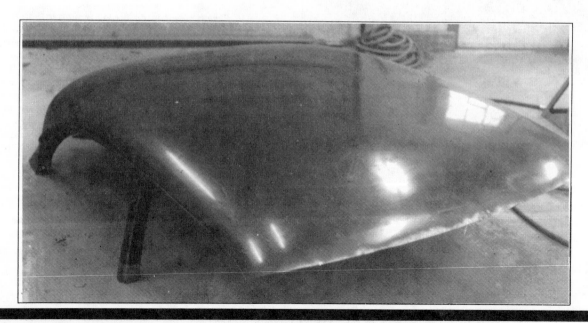

The trimmed original Buick top skin was cut to fit the bar stock atop the door glass area and across the front at the windshield. At the quarter panel and rear glass area the skin was clamped temporarily in place while new sheetmetal panels were cut and formed. The quarter window area was blanked off, in the best coachbuilder tradition, which adds to the low look of a chopped top. Berg did all the metal forming by hand.

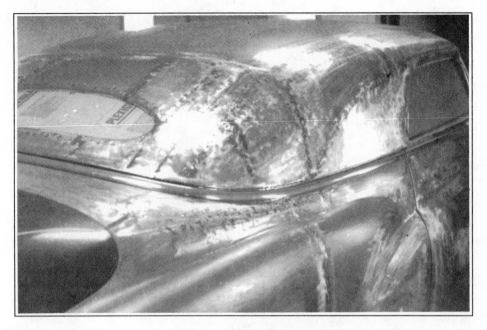

Once all the shaped panels were in place on the top, and the skin was welded to the tubing/bar stock perimeter bracing, the welds were finished and the top given a thin coat of plastic filler. The result was a super smooth foundation for the upholsterer, such a metal removable top could also be finished in paint. A metal overlay was made up for the deck lid and welded in place, this overlay carries through the theme of the hood on Buicks.

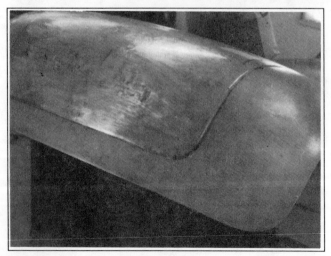

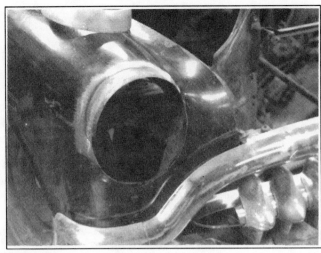

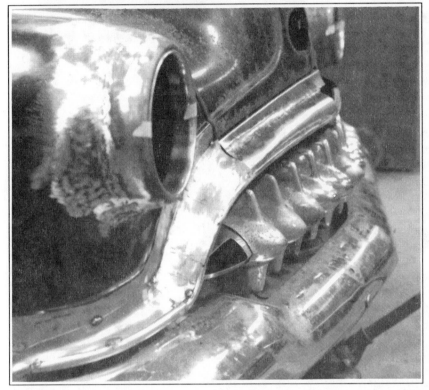

Headlights were extended slightly to include tunnel rings, the grille lip was stripped of chrome (by grinding) and tack welded to the fender. Note this upper grill surround has been cut apart in line with the original hood line, the parts will be molded to the fender to get a smooth, unbroken line. A floating grille bar was made up of Chevy pieces, everything was worked ultra smooth before getting to the platers.

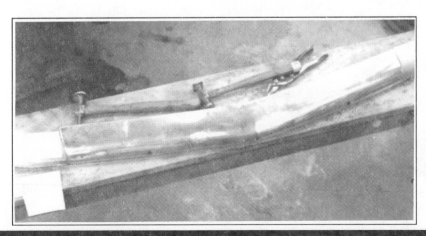

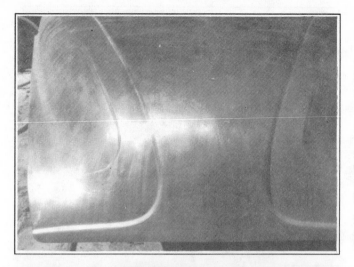

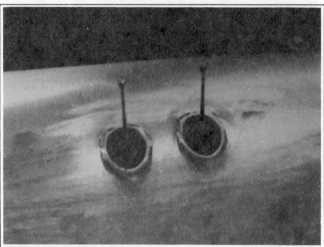

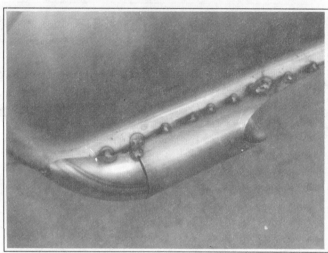

Dual antennas were frenched into the fenders, then some large diameter tubing was trimmed and welded to lower edge of front fenders as exit point for frenched side pipes. Small details that take a lot of time are what set the radical custom apart from the ordinary.

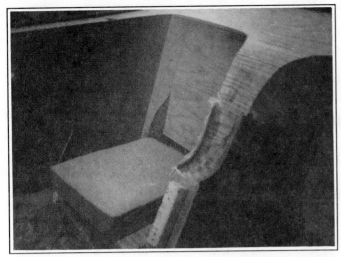

Rear set area was constructed of plywood fiberglassed into a base for padding and material, the front seats are pedestal style that seem originally as designed for the Buick. Superior craftsmanship in upholstery is apparent even to the casual observer of this car.

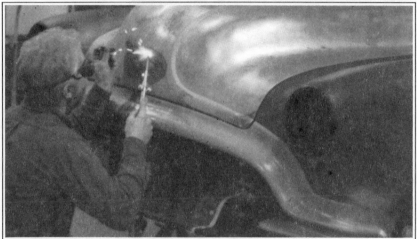

The Buick starting to take shape, with much of the modifications done and the body in grey primer. Berg welded the oval hood ornament opening shut, this time with a torch, then added some hammer welding to get a perfect surface. Working with a gas torch and then doing hammer welding is something that tends to identify a true craftsman in customizing.

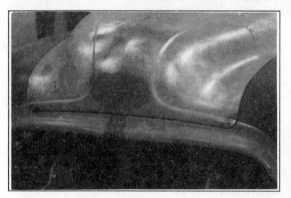

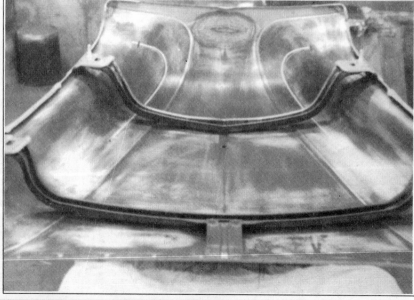

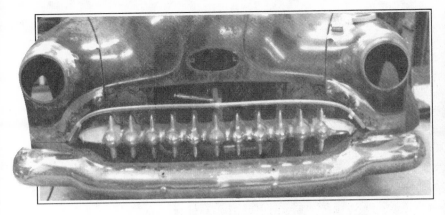

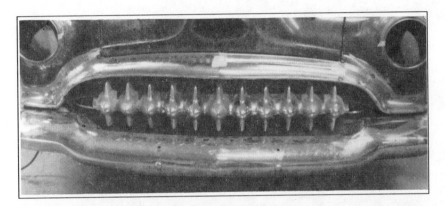

With outer sections of upper grille surround in place, and middle piece removed, a length of round stock is bent to shape and tacked to each side. Then the middle piece of surround below hood is tack-welded in place. Finally, everything is welded solid, and hood corners are rounded very slightly. Since the dechromed surround will be painted same color as the car, it will have minor amount of filler applied. Edge of original bumper is smoothed off, then all the pieces sent to chrome shop. This type of grille area modification can work as well on a mild custom as on a radical style change.

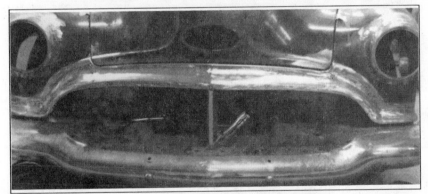

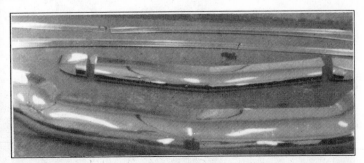

Metal top is upholstered/padded on the outside, interior upholstery theme is carried through the headliner. Several different ideas for special hubcaps were tried before the final design was adopted. Making up such a cap requires that all pieces be opposite each other to keep cap balanced, there are several suppliers of parts for anyone wishing to make a custom cap.

From left to right: Jim McFall, Upholsterer; M.K. John, Designer; Myrna Bozarth, Owner;
Ray Bozarth, Owner; Merlin Berg, Builder

LIST OF MODIFICATIONS ON '51 BUICK

1. NOSED & DECKED
2. DOOR HANDLES REMOVED
3. METAL SCALLOPS HAMMERED INTO HOOD
4. FENDER LINE ALTERED
5. HAND FORMED SCOOP WITH '53 MERC, TEETH
6. SHORTENED & LOWERED '53 BUICK SIDE MOULDINGS (LOWER AREA IS BUSHED FINISH)
7. FABRICATED METAL FENDER SKIRTS WITH ROLLED LOWER EDGE TO MATCH LOWER BODY LINE
8. GAS FILLER REMOVED FROM QUARTER AND INSTALLED IN TRUNK
9. GAS FILLER DOOR WELDED SHUT
10. EXTENDED QUARTERS
11. '55 PACKARD CLIPPER TAILLIGHTS
12. EXTENDED & ROLLED REAR PAN
13. '55 PONTIAC REAR BUMPER
14. FRONT FENDER PORT HOLES FILLED
15. FENDER EXTENDED INTO MERC. HEADLIGHT BEZELS
16. GRILL OPENING MOULDED IN WITH METAL & TUBE
17. '53 CHEVY GRILL WITH HAND MADE PARKING LIGHT ENDS
18. '51 BUICK FRONT BUMPER (MODIFIED)
19. TWO SUNKEN ANTENNAS
20. WINDSHIELD CHOPPED 3 1/2 INCHES
21. VENT WINDOWS REMOVED (ONE PIECE SIDE GLASS)
22. FABRICATED METAL REMOVABLE CARSON TOP
23. PASSENGER COMPARTMENT SHORTENED BY 7 INCHES AT THE UPPER DECK PANEL
24. HIDEAWAY FRONT LICENSE PLATE
25. '56 DODGE LANCER WHEEL COVERS (MODIFIED) '58 OLDS BLADES - GENE WINFIELD BULLETS
26. 350 CHEVY ENGINE
27. '73 CHEVY NOVA FRONT END
28. '75 MONTE CARLO REAR CROSS MEMBER & AXLE ASSEMBLY
29. LOWERED 6 INCHES
30. '75 MONTE CARLO TILT STEERING COLUMN
31. 350 CHEVY AUTOMATIC TRANSMISSION
32. AIR CONDITIONING
33. FRONT DOOR LENGTHENED 7 INCHES
34. DOOR POST MOVED BACK
35. BACK DOOR WELDED SHUT
36. ROUNDED HOOD CORNERS
37. CUSTOM BUILT BACK SEAT WITH FULL LENGTH FREE FLOATING ARM REST
38. MONTE CARLO SWIVEL FRONT SEATS (CUT DOWN)
39. LOWERED FLOOR
40. POWER STEERING
41. FRENCHED IN 81 INCH LAKE PIPES
42. '51 BUICK 2 DOOR BELTLINE CHROME
43. AXLE HUMP RAISED
44. NEW HAND FABRICATED DRIVE SHAFT TUNNEL
45. NEW RAISED & CONTOURED LINE ON THE TRUNK
46. TINTED SIDE WINDOWS
47. POWER ANTENNA
48. SPOTLIGHTS
49. ADJUSTERS - REAR SPRING
50. AIR SHOCKS

Construction Zone: '57 Plymouth

The Plymouth is not one of the most popular platforms for a custom, but as this hardtop shows, it is something that can be modified very well. In this case, the vehicle started with was in better than average condition. Torsion bar front suspension is a plus, since it allows the front to be dropped significantly.

by Jeff Soper

The 1957 Plymouth 2-door hardtop has always been my first love, ever since seeing one at a new car premier in '57. It was sleeker, wider, and lower than any of the new cars that year. My dad thought so too, and bought one with the 4bbl "power pack" engine and dual exhaust.

I bugged him for months until he finally let me lower it and put a set of Chris needlenose bubble skirts on. Even then, I knew this was a car that would make a fantastic "all out" custom.

In subsequent years, I owned two '57s, and dated my wife in dad's car. So, I knew it was fate a number of years ago when I found a '57 Plymouth in California (thanks to Hemmings). We flew to Los Angeles. 4000 miles later it was in my Ontario, Canada home. The odometer showed just 38,000 miles, so I didn't consider making it into a custom until the engine eventually threw a rod.

For 10 years the car sat in storage, while I gathered parts and made plans. During that time, I picked up a new 340 Mopar engine, 727A automatic trans, and '70 'Cuda axle and got stuff tentatively in place. Then things got in high gear.

Last year I attended the KKOA Leadsled Nats. Originally, I envisioned the car as a '50s custom, with the usual dechroming, louvered hood, '57 DeSoto chrome grille bar bumpers, '59 Plymouth front lower pan, and a tube grille. A pair of '57 Chrysler taillights and a rolled rear pan, lakes pipes and '57 Lancer hubcaps would have topped it off. But I went to the nats, and later I met Canadian customizer Jim Baille at a local cruise night. After tossing around some design ideas, the car was moved to Jim's shop to begin life as an '80s cruiser.

The first order of business was to chop the top 2 inches. Before starting any cutting, the doors were tack-welded shut and a frame of 1/2-inch tubing was braced in the rear window opening. Also, two legs of a support were tacked to the cowl panel, on the inside. Next the tricky part started.

The cowl was cut, just behind the firewall face in a horizontal line from firewall to rear edge of the windshield post. The cut must not interfere with the windshield wiper recesses, and the cut is made so that the cowl area will drop straight down. This is being done so that the windshield and back glass do not need to be cut.

Cut across the roof about 2 1/2 inches above the window, and down the center of each "C" post. Then cut around the rear deck panel about 1/2-inch away from the rear window opening. Cutting the remaining halves of the rear "C" post will free the roof, allowing the complete unit to be lowered as a single piece. The remaining rear window assembly, after trimming for fit, can then be moved forward slightly, under the roof skin, then welded. Once this is done, there are spaces between the firewall and cowl, and between the rear window surround and rear deck panel. Metal is handformed to fit and welded in place. When the dashboard is put back in place it will attach to the same screw holes, but will be 2 inches lower. At this time, a roof scoop was fabricated above the rear window for a third brake light.

The chrome trim on the rear fender fins and around the trunk area were removed, with the tops of the fins formed from metal into peaks. The gas filler door, fuel filler tube, and housing were removed and a patch welded in place. The gas filler will be located behind the license plate.

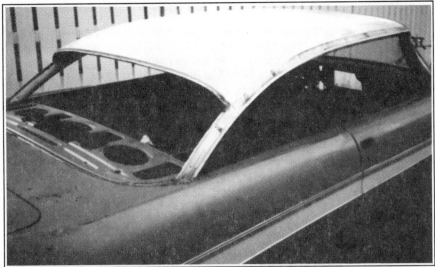

All the chrome trim around the top was removed, glass taken out before any cutting was done. Headliner was also removed from top and door-quarter panel upholstery was removed. If seats are taken out it gives more room to get around inside.

Before any cutting was done on the top, bracing was added to the stock rear window opening. Note that an angle meter is set on one of the braces, this is so the stock angle can be duplicated when the window area is set back in place. Cuts around area are as noted in chapter on top chopping.

The taillight backing plates were cut away and recessed housings were fabricated to fit the trimmed 1957 Chrysler taillight lens. They are tunneled about 5 inches into the fenders. The lower edges of the new housings were lined up parallel with the bottom edge of the trunk lid closure, and the rolled apron under the closure was extended to both sides (under the taillight housings to form platforms. The ends of these platforms were turned back into the apron to join the rear inside edge of the fender fin. the center apron section was cut out and new formed metal added. An inverted 1957 DeSoto grille bar was narrowed, the "V" straightened by cutting and realigning the end caps, and about 3 inches cut out of the back of the bumper. This leaves about 1 1/2-inches of the front lip. Each half of the bumper was then trimmed to make a tight fit against the lower apron lip. The end pieces were sectioned about 4 inches, with the cut-off cap spread and ballpeened to shape, then refitted to the bumper. All this to get a tight fit against the body.

After welding and finishing the end caps, the bumper halves were tack welded for alignment, then permanently welded to the lower pan lip and the quarter panels.

A license plate frame was made (over a wooden buck), and positioned in the center of the lower rear grille bar. A new lower pan was fabricated on each side under the bumper from quarters to the license frame, then welded to the bumper lower lip and license frame housing. The gas tank filler access is behind the license. A 1x4-inch recess was fabricated and welded into each end of the apron, under the taillight platforms, to allow mounting of a 3 or 4 bar tubular chrome grille.

To finish off the trunk area the lower deck lid corners were trimmed at an angle to match the inside angle of the rear fin, all chrome trim was removed, and an electric latch installed.

A new firewall was fabricated and welded over the original to give a smooth appearance, the only items mounted to this wall are the steering gear and brake booster. The heater/AC and all normal firewall-mounted components will be located inside the firewall, while cables, hoses, etc will route behind new inner fender splash aprons.

The front sheetmetal clip was bolted in place and the unusual flip-up "hood" was made. The lower body side moldings on the fenders were removed. A line was scribed along the bottom edge of the upper body side molding (on the fender) from the door to the front of the fender. The molding was removed and the top half of the fender cut along this scribed line, this cut was stopped 1-inch ahead of the door (temporary). At this time, the new splash aprons were formed of sheetmetal, attaching to the lower half of the fenders. The "loose" top piece of fender was aligned and temporarily tack welded into place with 1/8-inch rods as support.

The hood hinge assembly and supports were made of 1x2-inch thin wall steel tubing. A horizontal hood bar was cut and mounted at the front of the hood, welded at each end to the hood front corner reinforcements. This bar was aligned so that the rear edge of the bar was directly above the front face of the radiator yoke. The hood hinge support structure was placed directly below this bar, and against the face of the radiator yoke. This made the two structures aligned, allowing space for two steel butt hinges between them. The vertical bars of this support structure stand on the frame bumper support horns and are welded to both frame and radiator yoke. After alignment, the hinge halves were welded in place, completing the system.

The hood and upper fender halves were welded together, using 1/8-inch rod as a space filler between the hood and fenders. Now, that 1-inch remaining at the separation point between fender halves was cut (at the door jamb), and the cut was carried around the front of the fenders, up and over the headlight eyebrows, then to the hood edge. This frees the fender from the headlight bucket area. Now the entire fender/hood unit can be lifted off and the tops of the inner splash aprons can be welded in place, firewall to headlight bucket.

Top section of the radiator yoke was trimmed off, since none of this hood latch assembly area will be used.

After trimming the right and left bumper filler pan edges, another inverted 1957 DeSoto grill bar was tack welded in place. A matching center bumper filler was fabricated between radiator support and bumper. Grille bar ends were sectioned, spread, and reattached so that they are about l-inch ahead of the wheel opening lip, new lower front pan/air dam was molded to

the grille bar lower part, the corners rolled to meet the sides.

Rear of the hood was extended about 4 inches, and flaired up to the windshield. This covers the wipers same as new cars, but leaves plenty of wiper operation room. Top front edges of the doors were flaired to match the hood line. After installing the headlights (new quad units) to the bulkhead, a new peaked headlamp surround was made to fill the a gap between lights and upper fender/hood area. This was welded in place and swings up and away from the lights when the hood is opened.

The grille is made of 5/8-inch mild steel thin wall tubing. Finally, a functional set of 2-inch side pipes will be incorporated into the rocker panels. Built into these pipes will be mufflers.

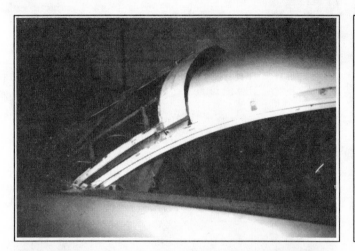

The rear window has been cut away from the top above and alongside the rear glass. At the front, the top is cut away below the windshield and entire top, including windshield and posts, is dropped straight down into the cowl area. On a wraparound windshield, the amount of drop may be limited by the dogleg in the door. At the rear of top, section that contacts quarter panel is trimmed until the drop is consistent fore/aft.

ADDITIONAL FEATURES

- Dual slanted antennas, mounted in an oval, peaked, raised, housing at upper corner of deck lid area.
- Radiused rear door corners.
- Upper side molding permanently welded to body, radius filled.
- Shaved door handles, solenoid operated doors.
- Electric hood latch recessed in cowl top.
- Molded windsplits on front fender tops.
- Floating 1-inch chrome tubes in front and rear bumper grille openings, lucite ends for hidden bulbs.
- Frame to have approximately 3 1/2 inches ground clearance, total car height 48-49 inches.
- 1980 Roadrunner wheels.
- Hood with 8 rows of louvers, underhood aluminum drain pan.
- Color to be super white acrylic enamel with graphics.
- Interior to be '70s-80s style.
- 1987 Daytona tilt steering wheel shaft.
- 1989 Daytona leather steering wheel.
- 1987 Dodge 600 wiper motor and assembly.
- 1980 Cordoba window lift slides and attachments.
- 1988 Ford electric window motor and arm assemblies.
- One-piece windows, vents eliminated.
- Sliding quarter windows.
- 1987 Daytona dual electric mirrors (Aero).
- 1987 Daytona interior flush door handles.
- 1987 Daytona emergency brake pedal.
- 1968 Charger fuel filler tube adapted to stock gas tank.
- New Direct Connection battery kit in trunk.

Area below rear window is cut away so glass can be slid forward, metal above glass is trimmed until it conforms to top shape, everything is then tack welded in place. Section below/behind rear window is then filled with sheet metal. It is possible, also, to drop rear window into a recess, same as front glass, to avoid having to cut the glass.

The top photo shows sheet metal that has been added to the recess area of windshield, this entire area is covered by extended hood (same as new cars with hideaway windshield wipers). Inner support structure for the rear window should be retained and rewelded to the repositioned top, this gives strength in a critical area.

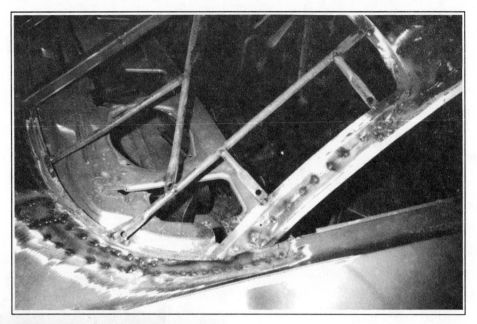

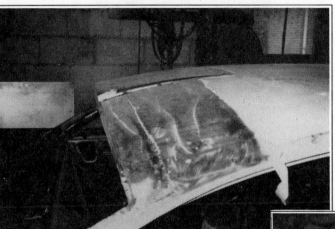

As usual, all the metal is tack welded in place so it can be checked for fit before any final welding is done. Here, the rear window support bracing can be removed after tack welding to check for glass fit before final welding. A third brake light roof scoop can be built from sheet stock, in this case the Plymouth fins were accentuated by adding sheet metal to the fin top edges.

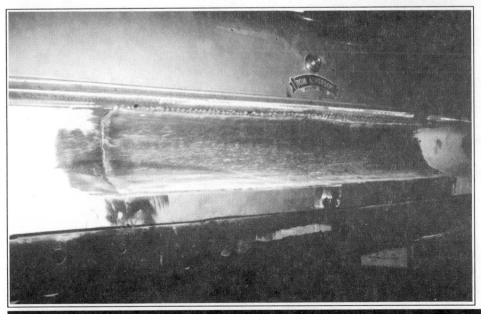

Stock Plymouth lights were semi-frenched, the buckets were dropped in even more to accentuate the tunnel look. The lower pan was radically reworked with sheet metal so that a frenched opening could be included to match the grille cavity in front.

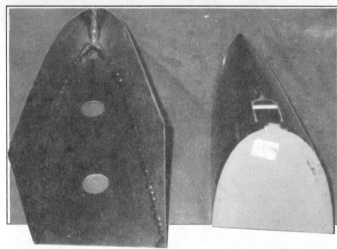

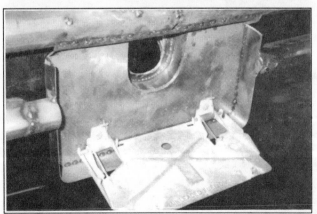

The MoPars seem to accept hooded headlights and tunneled taillights very well. The fenders were welded to the hood, slit lengthwise, and the entire top section tilts up. This is somewhat different that most tilt front ends. Gas filler is hidden behind the fold-down license plate.

After the tilt front end was created, the firewall and all inner splash panels were made up from flat sheet stock. In this area, spot welds are probably just as good as solid welds, no strength is hampered.

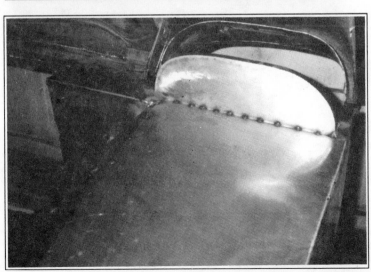

When the headlights and grille bars are installed, and the car is put on the ground, this will be one very unique custom. It is full of radical changes, yet the overall impression will be very subtle.

Pro Sled Extreme!

Sketch 1

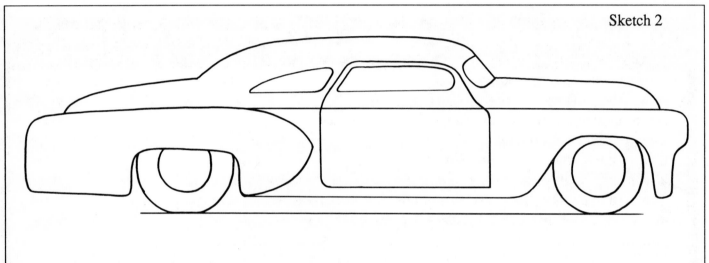

Sketch 2

By Ken Young

E ach and every time I build a custom car, I promise myself that I'll make it easier to build...and each time I end up with something more difficult than ever. This current project is the most radical car I've ever built. It has been a four year thrash, with all the typical stuff to tax the imagination and flex the talents.

Even so, I am strictly an amateur, so if I can do this, lots of other people can too. A MIG welder and plastic filler are my constant companions. Most of all, it was simply a matter of careful planning, patient work, and desire to have something totally different. I have included a sketch, which was a scale drawing I made by enlarging a snapshot of the stock car (used an opaque projector, many libraries have them). Tracing paper was laid over this projection so that the way I could get a really good idea about proportions. When I was satisfied with the final sketch, I started work.

Somewhat unusual is the top chop on this Chevy, in that the top has been lowered more than the average, and it has been split down the middle front to rear. A plywood buck was made that conforms to the top curvature, and this buck raised to hold the two top halves in place during preliminary welding. After the top was welded back in place, the body was removed from the chassis and a section taken all around. Note the square cut at rear wheel opening, so that opening lip could be raised in the fender.

During section process locating notches were cut into the door post area as an aid in alignment. The frame backbone is of 2x4 rectangular tubing, the body was on and off the basic frame several times during initial construction stages. A project of this type takes hundreds of hours, and a great deal of trial and error fitting.

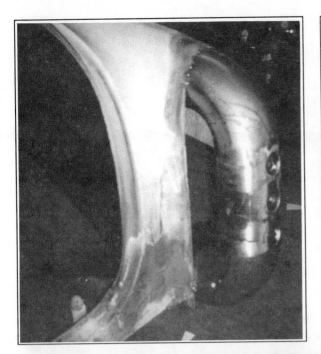

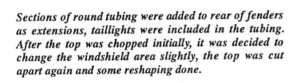

Sections of round tubing were added to rear of fenders as extensions, taillights were included in the tubing. After the top was chopped initially, it was decided to change the windshield area slightly, the top was cut apart again and some reshaping done.

This is a really radical departure from the normal custom. The square tubing frame includes room for narrow pro-street style rear end. Many racing items are included in the car making it much more like a Nascar tracker than a cruising streeter.

And for such a dramatic pro-sled, this one even includes an air conditioner. Electric fan mounts ahead of the radiator, extra oil radiators are outboard in front. The grille opening is a frenched piece of tubing, the bumper has been narrowed considerably, a hydraulic slave opens the tilt front sheet metal.

The interior takes on a very utilitarian appearance with flat dash and strictly-for-business gauges. This contrasts sharply with the button-tuft upholstery. Two-tone color combination of white and blue is another departure from tradition.

This book is dedicated to every custom car builder who has ever skinned a knuckle, burned a finger, or dropped an irreplaceable part. In short, it is for us all!